SHAKESPEARE

HAMLET

NOTES

COLES EDITORIAL BOARD

A NOTE TO THE READER

These Notes present a clear discussion of the action and thought of the work under consideration and a concise interpretation of its artistic merits and its significance.

They are intended as a supplementary aid to the serious student. They serve to free the student from interminable and distracting note-taking in class so that he may listen intelligently to what the instructor is saying, or to the class discussion, making selective notes on these, secure in the knowledge that he has the basic understanding. They are also helpful in preparing for an examination, saving not merely the burden but the confusion of trying to re-read the full text under pressure, and disentangling from a mass of — often illegible — notes that which is of central importance.

THE NOTES ARE NOT A SUBSTITUTE FOR THE TEXT ITSELF OR FOR THE CLASSROOM DISCUSSION OF THE TEXT, AND THE STUDENT WHO SO ATTEMPTS TO USE THEM IS DENYING HIMSELF THE VERY EDUCATION THAT HE IS PRESUMABLY GIVING HIS MOST VITAL YEARS TO ACHIEVE.

The critical evaluations have been prepared by experts with special knowledge of the individual texts who have usually had some years' experience in teaching the works. They are, however, not incontrovertible. No literary judgment is. Of any great work of literature there are many interpretations, and even conflicting views have value for the student (and the teacher), since the aim is not for the student to accept unquestioningly any one interpretation but to make his own.

0 - 7740 - 3193 - X

©COPYRIGHT 1985 AND PUBLISHED BY
COLES PUBLISHING COMPANY LIMITED
TORONTO — CANADA
PRINTED IN CANADA

CONTENTS

WILLIAM SHAKESPEARE: LIFE AND WORKS

Biographical Sketch

The Early Years

Despite the scholarship it has generated, our knowledge of Shakespeare's life is sketchy, filled with more questions than answers, even after we discard the misinformation accumulated over the years. He was baptized on April 26, 1564, in Holy Trinity Church, Stratford-on-Avon. As it was customary to baptize children a few days after birth, he was probably born on April 23. The monument erected in Stratford states that he died on April 23, 1616, in his fifty-third year.

William was the third child of John Shakespeare, who came to Stratford from Snitterfield before 1532 as a "whyttawer" (tanner) and glover, and Mary Arden, daughter of a wealthy "gentleman of worship" from Wilmecote. They married around 1557. Since John Shakespeare owned one house on Greenhill Street and two on Henley Street, we cannot be certain where William was born, though the Henley Street shrine draws many tourists each year. William's two older sisters died in infancy, but three brothers and two other sisters survived at least into childhood.

Shakespeare's father was well-to-do, dealing in farm products and wool, and owning considerable property in Stratford. After holding a series of minor municipal offices he was elected alderman in 1565, high bailiff (roughly similar to the mayor of today) in 1568, and chief alderman in 1571. There are no records of young Will Shakespeare's education (though there are many unfounded legends), but he probably attended the town school maintained by the burgesses, which prepared its students for the universities. Ben Jonson's line about Shakespeare's having "small *Latine*, and lesse *Greeke*" refers not to his education but to his lack of indebtedness to the classical writers and dramatists.

On November 27, 1582, a licence to marry was issued to "Willelmum Shaxpere *et* Annam Whateley *de* Temple Grafton." On the next day a marriage bond for "Willm Shagspere" and "Anne Hathwey of Stratford" was signed by Fulk Sandells and John Richardson, farmers of Stratford. This bond stated that there was no "lawful let or impediment by reason of any precontract, consanguinity, affinity, or by any other lawful means whatsoever"; thus "William and Anne (were) to be married together with once asking of the banns of matrimony." The problem of Anne Whateley has led many researchers to argue all kinds of improbabilities, such as the existence of two different Shakespeares and the forging of documents to conceal Shakespeare's true identity. The actual explanation seems to be simple: the clerk who made the marriage licence entry apparently copied the name "Whateley" from a preceding entry, as a glance at the full sheet suggests. (Incidentally, Nicholas Rowe in his life of Shakespeare, published in 1709, well before the discovery of these marriage records, gave Anne's name as Hathaway.) The problems of marriage with Anne Hathaway — he was eighteen and she was twenty-six — and of the bond have caused similar consternation. Why did these two marry when there was such a discrepancy of age? Why only one saying of the banns (rather than the usual three)? Why the emphasis on a possible legal problem? The answer here is not simple or definite, but the birth of a daughter Susanna, baptized at Holy Trinity on May 26, 1583, seems to explain the odd circumstances. It should be recognized, however, that an engagement to marry was considered legally binding in those days (we still have breach-of-promise suits today) and that premarital relations were not unusual or frowned upon when an engagement had taken place. The circumstances already mentioned, Shakespeare's ensuing activities, and his will bequeathing to Anne "my second best bed with the furniture" have suggested to some that their marriage was not entirely happy. Their other children, the twins Hamnet and Judith, were christened on February 2, 1585.

Theatrical Life

Shakespeare's years before and immediately after the time of his marriage are not charted, but rumor has him as an apprentice to a master butcher or as a country teacher or an actor with some provincial company. He is supposed to have run away from whatever he was doing for livelihood and to have gone to London, where he soon joined a theatrical group. At this time there were only two professional houses established in London, The Theatre (opened in 1576) and The Curtain (opened in 1577). His first connection with the theater was reputedly as holder of horses; that is, one of the stage crew, but a most inferior assignment. Thereafter he became an actor (perhaps at this time he met Ben Johnson), a writer, and a director. Such experience had its mark in the theatricality of his plays. We do know that he was established in London by 1592, when Robert Greene lamented in *A Groatsworth of Wit* (September, 1592) that professional actors had gained priority in the theater over university-trained writers like himself: "There is an upstart Crow, beautified with our feathers, that with his *Tygers hart wrapt in a Players hyde,* supposes he is as well able to bombast out a lanke verse as the best of you: and beeing an absolute *Iohannes fac totum* (Jack-of-all-trades), is in his owne conceit the onely Shake-scene in a countrey." An apology for Greene's ill-humored statement by Henry Chettle, the editor of the pamphlet, appeared around December 1592 in *Kind-Hart's Dream.*

Family Affairs

To return to the known details of his family life, Shakespeare's

2

son Hamnet was buried at Stratford on August 11, 1596; his father was given a coat of arms on October 20, 1596; and Will purchased New Place (a refurbished tourist attraction today) on May 4, 1597. The London playwright obviously had not severed connections with his birthplace, and he was reflecting his new affluence by being known as William Shakespeare of Stratford-upon-Avon, in the County of Warwick, Gentleman. His father was buried in Stratford on September 8, 1601; his mother, on September 9, 1608. His daughter Susanna married Dr. John Hall on June 5, 1607, and they had a child named Elizabeth. His other daughter, Judith, married Thomas Quiney on February 10, 1616, without special licence, during Lent and was thus excommunicated. Shakespeare revised his will on March 25, 1616, and was buried on April 25, 1616 (according to the parish register). A monument by Gerard Janssen was erected in the Holy Trinity chancel in 1623 but many, like Milton several years later, protested:

> What needs my *Shakespeare* for his honour'd Bones,
> The labour of an age in piled Stone, . . .
> Thou in our wonder and astonishment
> Hast built thy self a live-long Monument.

Shakespeare's Writings

Order of Appearance

Dating of Shakespeare's early plays, while based on inconclusive evidence, has tended to hover around the early 1590s. Almost certainly, it is his chronicles of Henry the Sixth that Philip Henslowe, an important theatrical manager of the day, referred to in his diary as being performed during March-May, 1592. An allusion to these plays also occurs in Thomas Nashe's *Piers Penniless His Supplication to the Devil* (August, 1592).

The first published work to come from Shakespeare's hand was *Venus and Adonis* (1593), a long poem, dedicated to Henry Wriothesley, Earl of Southampton. A year later *The Rape of Lucrece* appeared, also dedicated to Southampton. Perhaps poetry was pursued during these years because the London theaters were closed as a result of an outbreak of plague. The *Sonnets*, published in 1609, may owe something to Southampton, who had become Shakespeare's patron. Perhaps some were written as early as the first few years of the 1590's. They were mentioned (along with a number of plays) in 1598 by Francis Meres in his *Palladis Tamia*, and sonnets 138 and 144 were printed without authority by William Jaggard in *The Passionate Pilgrim* (1599).

There is a record of a performance of *A Comedy of Errors* at Gray's Inn (one of the law colleges) on December 28, 1594, and,

3

during early 1595, Shakespeare was paid, along with the famous actors Richard Burbage and William Kempe, for performances before the Queen by the Lord Chamberlain's Men, a theatrical company formed the year before. The company founded the Globe Theatre in 1599 and became the King's Men when James ascended the throne. Records show frequent payments to the company through its general manager John Heminge. From 1595 through 1614 there are numerous references to real estate transactions and other legal matters, to many performances, and to various publications connected with Shakespeare.

Order of Publication

The first plays to be printed were *Titus Andronicus* around February, 1594, and the garbled versions of *Henry VI*, Parts II and III in 1594. Thereafter *Richard III* appeared in 1597 and 1598; *Richard II*, in 1597 and twice in 1958; *Romeo and Juliet*, in 1597 (a pirated edition) and 1599, and many others. Some of the plays appear in individual editions, with or without Shakespeare's name on the title page, but eighteen are known only from their appearance in the first collected volume (the so-called First Folio) of 1623. The editors were Heminge and Henry Condell, another member of Shakespeare's company. *Pericles* was omitted from the First Folio although it had appeared in 1609, 1611, and 1619; it was added to the Third Folio in 1664.

There was reluctance to publish plays at this time for various reasons; many plays were carelessly written for fast production; collaboration was frequent; plays were not really considered *reading* matter; they were sometimes circulated in manuscript; and the theatrical company, not the author, owned the rights. Those plays given individual publication appeared in a quarto, so named from the size of the page. A single sheet of paper was folded twice to make four leaves (thus *quarto*) or eight pages; these four leaves constitute one signature (one section of a bound book). A page measures about 6-3/4 in. × 8-1/2 in. On the other hand, a folio sheet is folded once to make two leaves or four pages; three sheets, or twelve pages, constitute a signature. The page is approximately 8-1/2 in. × 13-3/4 in.

Authorized publication occurred when a company disbanded, when money was needed but rights were to be retained, when a play failed or ran into licensing difficulties (thus, hopefully, the printed work would justify the play against the criticism), or when a play had been pirated. Authorized editions are called good quartos. Piratical publication might occur when the manuscript of a play had circulated privately, when a member of a company desired money for himself, or when a stenographer or memorizer took the play down in the theater (such a version was recognizable by inclusion of stage directions derived from an eyewitness, by garbled sections, etc.). Pirated editions are called bad quartos; there are at least five bad quartos of Shakespeare's plays.

Authenticity of Works

Usually thirty-seven plays are printed in modern collections of Shakespeare's works but some recent scholars have urged the addition of two more: *Edward III* and *Two Noble Kinsmen*. At times, six of the generally-accepted plays have been questioned: *Henry I,* Parts I, II and III, *Timon of Athens, Pericles* and *Henry VIII*. The first four are usually accepted today (one hopes all question concerning *Timon* has finally ended), but if Shakespeare did not write these plays in their entirety, he certainly wrote parts of them. Of course, collaboration in those days was common. Aside from the two long narrative poems already mentioned and the sonnets (Nos. 1-152, but not Nos. 153-154), Shakespeare's poetic output is uncertain. *The Passionate Pilgrim* (1599) contains only five authenticated poems (two sonnets and three verses from *Love's Labour's Lost*); *The Phoenix and the Turtle* (1601) may be his, but the authenticity of *A Lover's Complaint* (appended to the sonnets) is highly questionable.

Who Was Shakespeare?

At this point we might mention a problem that has plagued Shakespeare study for over a century: who was Shakespeare? Those who would like to make the author of the plays someone else — Francis Bacon or the Earl of Oxford or even Christopher Marlowe (dead long before most of the plays were written) — have used the lack of information of Shakespeare's early years and the confusion in the evidence we have been examining to advance their candidate. But the major arguments against Shakespeare show the source of these speculators' disbelief to be in classconscious snobbery and perhaps in a perverse adherence to minority opinion. The most common argument is that no one of Shakespeare's background, lack of education, and lack of aristocratic experience could know all that the author knew. But study will reveal that such information was readily available in various popular sources, that some of it lies in the literary sources used for the play, and that Shakespeare was probably not totally lacking in education or in social decorum. The more significant question of style and tone is not dealt with — nor could it successfully be raised. Bacon, for example, no matter how much we admire his mind and his writings, exhibits a writing style diametrically opposite to Shakespeare's, a style most unpoetic and often flat. The student would be wise not to waste time rehashing these unfounded theories. No such question was raised in the seventeenth or eighteenth centuries, and no serious student of the plays today doubts that Shakespeare *was* Shakespeare.

Shakespeare's Plays

Exact dates for Shakespeare's plays remain a source of debate among scholars. The following serve only as a general frame of reference.

COMEDIES	TRAGEDIES	HISTORIES
1591		Henry VI, Part I
1592 Comedy of Errors		Henry VI, Part II
1592 Two Gentlemen of Verona		Henry VI, Part III
1593 Love's Labour's Lost	Titus Andronicus	Richard III
1594		King John
1595 Midsummer Night's Dream	Romeo and Juliet	Richard II
1596 Merchant of Venice		
1596 Taming of the Shrew		
1597		Henry IV, Part I
1598 Much Ado About Nothing		Henry IV, Part II
1599 As You Like It	Julius Caesar	
1599 Merry Wives of Windsor		Henry V
1601 Twelfth Night	Hamlet	
1602 Troilus and Cressida		
1602 All's Well That Ends Well		
1604 Measure for Measure	Othello	
1605	King Lear	
1606	Macbeth	
1607	Timon of Athens	
1607	Antony and Cleopatra	
1608 Pericles		
1609	Coriolanus	
1610 Cymbeline		
1611 Winter's Tale		
1611 Tempest		
1613		Henry VIII

Shakespeare's England

The world of Elizabethan and Jacobean England was a world of growth and change. The great increase in the middle class, and in the population as a whole, demanded a new economy and means of livelihood, a new instrument of government (one recognizing "rights" and changed class structure), a new social code and a broad base of entertainment. The invention of printing a century before had contributed to that broader base, but it was the theater that supplied the more immediate needs of the greatest numbers. The theater grew and along with it came less-educated, more money-conscious writers, who gave the people what they wanted: entertainment. But Shakespeare, having passed through a brief period of hack writing, proceeded to set down important ideas in memorable language throughout most of his career. His plays, particularly the later ones, have been analyzed by recent critics in terms of literary quality through their metaphor, verse-line, relationships with psychology and myth, and elaborate structure. Yet Shakespeare was a man of the stage, and the plays were written to be performed. Only this will fully account for the humor of a deadly serious play like *Hamlet* or the spectacle of a *Coriolanus.*

Life in London

During Shakespeare's early years there, London was a walled city of about 200,000, with seven gates providing access to the city from the east, north and west. It was geographically small and crisscrossed by narrow little streets and lanes. The various wards each had a parish church that dominated the life of the close-knit community. To the south and outside were slums and the haunts of criminal types, and farther out were the agricultural lands and huge estates. As the population increased and the central area declined, the fashionable people of the city moved toward the west, where the palace of Westminster lay. Houses were generally rented out floor by floor and sometimes room by room. Slums were common within the city, too, though close to pleasant enough streets and squares. "Merrie Olde England" was not really clean, nor were its people, for in those days there were no sewers or drains except the gutter in the middle of the street, into which garbage would be emptied to be floated off by the rain. Plague was particularly ravaging in 1592, 1593-94 (when the theaters were closed to avoid contamination) and 1603. Medical knowledge, of course, was slight; ills were "cured" by amputation, leeching and blood-letting. The city was (and still is) dominated by St. Paul's Cathedral, around which booksellers clustered on Paternoster Row.

Religious Atmosphere

Of great significance for the times was religion. Under Elizabeth, a state church had developed; it was Protestant in nature and was called Anglican (or today, Episcopalian). It had arisen from Henry VIII's break with the Pope and from a compromise with the Roman Catholics who had gained power under Mary Tudor.

The Church of England was headed by the Archbishop of Canterbury, who was to be an increasingly important figure in the early part of the seventeenth century. There were also many schismatic groups, which generally desired further departures from Roman Catholicism. Calvinists were perhaps the most numerous and important of the Protestant groups. The Puritans, who were Calvinist, wanted to "purify" the church of ritual and certain ideas, but during the 1590s they were labeled as extremists in dress and conduct.

Political Milieu

During Shakespeare's lifetime there were two monarchs: Elizabeth, 1558-1603, and James I, 1603-1625. Elizabeth was the daughter of Henry VIII and Anne Boleyn, his second wife, who was executed in 1536. After Henry's death, his son by his third wife, Jane Seymour (who died in 1537), reigned as Edward VI. He was followed by Mary Tudor, daughter of Henry's first wife, Catherine of Aragon. Mary was a Roman Catholic, who tried to put down religious dissension by persecution of both Protestants and Catholics. Nor did her marriage to Philip II of Spain endear her to the people.

Elizabeth's reign was troubled by many offers of marriage, particularly from Spanish and French nobles — all Roman Catholic — and by the people's concern for an heir to the throne. English suitors generally cancelled one another out by intrigue or aggressiveness. One of the most prominent was the Earl of Essex, Robert Devereux, who fell in and out of favor; he apparently attempted to take over the reins of control, only to be captured, imprisoned and executed in February, 1601. One claimant to the throne was Mary of Scotland, a Roman Catholic and widow of Francis II of France. She was the second cousin of Elizabeth, tracing her claim through her grandmother, who was Henry VIII's sister. Finally, settlement came with Elizabeth's acceptance of Mary's son as heir apparent, though Mary was to be captured, tried and executed for treason in 1587. Mary had abdicated the throne of Scotland in 1567 in favor of her son, James VI. His ascent to the throne of England in 1603 as James I joined the two kingdoms for the first time, although Scotland during the seventeenth century often acted independently of England.

Contemporary Events

Political and religious problems were intermingled in the celebrated Gunpowder Plot. Angry over fines that were levied upon those not attending Church of England services — primarily Roman Catholics — and offended by difficulties over papal envoys, a group of Catholics plotted to blow up Parliament, and James with it, at its first session on November 5, 1605. A cache of gunpowder was stored in the cellar, guarded by various conspirators, among them Guy Fawkes. The plot was discovered before it could be carried out and Fawkes, on duty at the time, was arrested. The execution of the plotters and the triumph of the anti-Papists led in succeeding years to celebrations in the streets and the hanging of Fawkes in effigy.

Among the most noteworthy public events during these times were the wars with the Spanish, which included the defeat of the Spanish Armada in 1588, the battle in the Lowlands in 1590-1594, the expedition to Cadiz under Essex in 1596 and the expedition to the Azores (the Islands Expedition), also under Essex, in 1597. With trading companies specially set up for colonization and exploitation, travel excited the imagination of the people: here was a new way of life, here were new customs brought back by the sailors and merchants, here was a new world to explore.

In all, the years from around 1590 to 1601 were trying ones for English people, relieved only by the news from abroad, the new affluence and the hope for the future under James. Writers of this period frequently reflect, however, the disillusionment and sadness of those difficult times.

The Elizabethan Theater

Appearance

The Elizabethan playhouse developed from the medieval inn with its rooms grouped around a courtyard into which a stage was built. This pattern was used in The Theatre, built by James Burbage in 1576: a square frame building (later round or octagonal) with a square yard, three tiers of galleries, each jutting out over the one below, and a stage extending into the middle of the yard, where people stood or sat on improvised seats. There was no cover over the yard or stage and lighting was therefore natural. Performances were held in the afternoon.

Other theaters were constructed over the years: The Curtain in 1577, The Rose in 1587 (on Bankside), The Swan in 1595 (also Bankside) and Shakespeare's playhouse, The Globe, in 1599 (not far from The Rose). There is still some question about the exact dimensions of this house, but it seems to have been octagonal, each side measuring about 36 feet, with an over-all diameter of 84 feet. It was about 33 feet to the eaves, and the yard was 56 feet in diameter. Three sides were used for backstage and to serve the needs of the players. The stage jutted out into the audience and there was no curtain. The spectators often became part of the action. Obviously, the actors' asides and soliloquies were effective under these conditions.

There was no real scenery and there were only a few major props. Thus the lines of the play had to reveal locations and movement, changes in time or place, etc. In this way, too, it was easier to establish a nonrealistic setting, for all settings were created in words. On either side of the stage were doors, within the flooring were trapdoors (for entrances of ghosts, etc.), and behind the main stage was the inner stage or recess. Here, indoor scenes (such as a court or a bedchamber) were played, and some props could be used because the inner stage was usually concealed by a curtain when not in use. It might also have served to hide someone behind the ever-present arras (hanging tapestry), like Polonius in *Hamlet*. The "chamber" was on the second level, with windows and a balcony. On the third level was another chamber, primarily for musicians.

Actors

An acting company such as the Lord Chamberlain's Men was a fellowship of ten to fifteen sharers with some ten to twelve extras, three or four boys (often to play women's roles) who might become full sharers, and stagehands. There were rival companies, each with its leading dramatist and leading tragic actor and clown. The Lord Admiral's Men, organized in 1594, boasted Ben Jonson and the tragedian Edward Alleyn. Some of the rivalry of this War of the Theaters is reflected in the speeches of Hamlet, who comments on the ascendancy and unwarranted popularity of the children's companies (like the Children of Blackfriars) in the late 1590s.

The company dramatist, of course, had to think in terms of the members of his company as he wrote his play. He had to make use of the physical features and peculiar talents of the actors, making sure, besides, that there was a role for each member. The fact that women's parts were taken by boys imposed obvious limitations on the range of action. Accordingly, we often find women characters impersonating men. For example, Robert Goffe played Portia in *The Merchant of Venice*, and Portia impersonates a male lawyer in the important trial scene. Goffe also played Juliet, and Anne in *Richard III*, and Oberon in *A Midsummer Night's Dream*. The influence of an actor on the playwright can be seen, on the one hand, by noting the "humor" characters portrayed so competently by Thomas Pope, who was a choleric Mercutio in *Romeo*, a melancholic Jaques in *As You Like It*, and a sanguinary Falstaff in *Henry IV*, Part I; and by comparing, on the other hand, the clown Bottom in *A Midsummer Night's Dream*, played in a frolicsome manner by William Kempe, with the clown Feste in *Twelfth Night*, sung and danced by Robert Armin. Obviously, too, if a certain kind of character was not available within the company, then that kind of character could not be written into the play. The approach was decidedly different from ours today, where the play almost always comes first and the casting of roles second. The plays were performed in a repertory system, with a different play each afternoon. The average life of a play was about ten performances.

History of the Drama

English drama goes back to native forms developed from playlets presented at Church holidays. Mystery plays dealt with biblical stories such as the Nativity or the Passion, and miracle plays usually depicted the lives of saints. The merchant and craft guilds that came to own and produce the cycles of plays were the forerunners of the theatrical companies of Shakespeare's time. The kind of production these cycles received, either as moving pageants in the streets or as staged shows in a churchyard, influenced the late sixteenth-century production of a secular play: there was an intimacy with the audience and there was a great reliance on words rather than setting and props. Similar involvement with the stage action is experienced by audiences of the arena theater of today.

The morality play, the next form to develop, was an allegory of the spiritual conflict between good and evil in the soul of man. The *dramatis personae* were abstract virtues and vices, with at least one man representing Mankind (or Everyman, as the most popular of these plays was titled). Some modern critics see *Othello* as a kind of morality play in which the soul of Othello is vied for by the aggressively evil Iago (as a kind of Satanic figure) and passively good Desdemona (as a personification of Christian faith in all men). The Tudor interlude — a short, witty, visual play — may have influenced the subplot of the Elizabethan play with its low-life and jesting and visual tricks. In mid-sixteenth century appeared the earliest known English comedies, Nicholas Udall's *Ralph Roister Doister* and *Gammer Gurton's Needle* (of uncertain authorship). Both show the influence of the Roman comic playwright Plautus. Shakespeare's *Comedy of Errors*, performed in the 1590's, was an adaptation of Plautus' *Menaechmi*, both plays featuring twins and an involved story of confused identities. The influence of the Roman tragedian Seneca can be traced from Thomas Norton and Thomas Sackville in *Gorboduc* to *Hamlet*. Senecan tragedy is a tragedy of revenge, characterized by many deaths, much blood-letting, ghosts, feigned madness and the motif of a death for a death.

Shakespeare's Artistry

Plots

Generally, a Shakespearean play has two plots: a main plot and a subplot. The subplot reflects the main plot and is often concerned with inferior characters. Two contrasting examples will suffice: Lear and his daughters furnish the characters for the main plot of filial love and ingratitude. Gloucester and his sons enact the same theme in the subplot. Lear and Gloucester both learn that outward signs of love may be false. In *A Midsummer Night's Dream*, the town workmen (Quince, Bottom *et al.*) put on a tragic play in such a hilarious way that it turns the subject of the play — love so strong that the hero will kill himself if his loved one dies first — into farce, but this in the main plot is the "serious" plight of the four mixed-up lovers. In both examples Shakespeare has reinforced his points by subplots dealing with the same subject as the main plot.

Sources

The plots of the Elizabethan plays were usually adapted from other sources. Originality was not the sought quality; a kind of variation on a theme was. It was felt that one could better evaluate the playwright's worth by seeing what he did with a familiar tale. What he stressed, how he stressed it, how he restructured the familiar elements — these were the important matters. Shakespeare closely followed Sir Thomas North's popular translation of Plutarch's *Life of Marcus*

Antonius, for example, in writing *Antony and Cleopatra.* He modified Robert Greene's *Pandosto* and combined it with the Pygmalion myth in *The Winter's Tale,* while drawing the character of Autolycus from certain pamphlets written by Greene. The only plays for which sources have not been clearly determined are *Love's Labour's Lost* (probably based on contemporary events) and *The Tempest* (possibly based on some shipwreck account from travelers to the New World).

Verse and Prose

There is a mixture of verse and prose in the plays, partially because plays fully in verse were out of fashion. Greater variety could thus be achieved and character or atmosphere could be more precisely delineated. Elevated passages, philosophically significant ideas, speeches by men of high rank are in verse, but comic and light parts, speeches including dialect or broken English, and scenes that move more rapidly or simply give mundane information are in prose. The poetry is almost always blank verse (iambic pentameter lines without rhyme). Rhyme is used, however (particularly the couplet), to mark the close of scenes or an important action. Rhyme also serves as a cue for the entrance of another actor or some off-stage business, to point to a change of mood or thought, as a forceful opening after a passage of prose, to convey excitement or passion or sentimentality and to distinguish characters.

Shakespeare's plays may be divided into three general categories, though some plays are not readily classified and further subdivisions may be suggested within a category.

The History Play

The history play, or chronicle, may tend to tragedy, like *Richard II,* or to comedy, like *Henry IV,* Part I. It is a chronicle of some royal personage, often altered for dramatic purposes, even to the point of falsifying the facts. Its popularity may have resulted from the rising of nationalism of the English, nurtured by their successes against the Spanish, their developing trade and colonization, and their rising prestige as a world power. The chronicle was considered a political guide, like the popular *Mirror for Magistrates,* a collection of writings showing what happens when an important leader falls through some error in his ways, his thinking or his personality. Thus the history play counsells the right path by negative, if not positive, means. Accordingly, it is difficult to call *Richard II* a tragedy, since Richard was wrong and his wrongness harmed his people. The political philosophy of Shakespeare's day seemed to favor the view that all usurpation was bad and should be corrected, but not by further usurpation. When that original usurpation had been established, through an heir's ascension to the throne, it was to be accepted. Then any rebellion against the "true" king would be a rebellion against God.

Tragedy

Tragedy, in simple terms, means that the protagonist dies. Certain concepts drawn from Aristotle's *Poetics* require a tragic hero of high standing, who must oppose some conflicting force, either external or internal. The tragic hero should be dominated by a *hamartia* (a so-called tragic flaw, but really an *excess* of some character trait, e.g., pride, or *hubris*), and it is this *hamartia* that leads to his downfall and, because of his status, to the downfall of others. The action presented in the tragedy must be recognizable to the audience as real. Through seeing it enacted, the audience has its passion (emotions) raised, and the conclusion of the action thus brings release from that passion (*catharsis*). A more meaningful way of looking at tragedy in the Elizabethan theater, however, is to see it as that which occurs when essential good (like Hamlet) is wasted (through disaster or death) in the process of driving out evil (such as Claudius represents).

Comedy

Comedy in simple terms means that the play ends happily for the protagonists. Sometimes the comedy depends on exaggerations of man's eccentricities — comedy of humors; sometimes the comedy is romantic and far-fetched. The romantic comedy was usually based on a mix-up in events or confused identity of characters, particularly by disguise. It moves towards tragedy in that an important person might die and the mix-up might never be unraveled; but in the nick of time something happens or someone appears (sometimes illogically or unexpectedly) and saves the day. It reflects the structure of myth by moving from happiness to despair to resurrection. *The Winter's Tale* is a perfect example of this, for the happiness of the first part is banished with Hermione's exile and Perdita's abandonment. Tragedy is near when the lost baby, Perdita, cannot be found and Hermione is presumed dead. But Perdita reappears, as does Hermione, a statue that suddenly comes to life. Lost identities are established and confusions disappear but the mythic-comic nature of the play is seen in the reuniting of the mother, Hermione, a kind of Ceres, with her daughter, Perdita, a kind of Proserpina. Spring returns, summer will bring the harvest, and the winter of the tale is left behind — for a little while.

What is it, then, that makes Shakespeare's art so great? Perhaps we see in it a whole spectrum of humanity, treated impersonally, but with kindness and understanding. We seldom meet in Shakespeare a weeping philosopher: he may criticize, but he criticizes both sides. After he has done so, he gives the impression of saying, Well, that's the way life is; people will always be like that — don't get upset about it. This is probably the key to the Duke's behavior in *Measure for Measure* — a most unbitter comedy despite former labels. Only in *Hamlet* does Shakespeare not seem to fit this statement; it is the one play that Shakespeare, the person, enters.

As we grow older and our range of experience widens, so, too, does Shakespeare's range seem to expand. Perhaps this lies in the ambiguities of his own materials, which allow for numerous individual readings. We meet our own experiences — and they are ours alone, we think — expressed in phrases that we thought our own or our own discovery. What makes Shakespeare's art so great, then, is his ability to say so much to so many people in such memorable language: he is himself "the show and gaze o' the time."

HAMLET

Introduction

One of the best known pieces of literature throughout the world, *Hamlet* is also accorded a position of high merit among the superior works of art. What has fascinated readers, scholars, critics, psychologists and actors is the character of Hamlet, the reasons for his actions or at times lack of action, and the relationships with his mother, uncle, and loved Ophelia. In addition, problems of text and source have allowed much room for speculation as to Shakespeare's intent and contribution to the legend or to the sub-genre of revenge tragedy. Recent criticism has attempted to view the play more completely through study of all characters, subplot, imagery and structure. Rather than the older view that the play deals only with the problem of man's relationship to himself, such criticism suggests a creation which delves into such universal problems as appearance and reality (what is called the double vision of life), and man's relationship to God.

Sources of the Play

Shakespearean experts are sure that Shakespeare's original source for his play *The Tragedy of Hamlet, Prince of Denmark* was a play on the same subject attributed to Thomas Kyd and performed in London before 1590. This play, whose manuscript has since disappeared, was called the *Ur-Hamlet*. Phillip Henslowe, an Elizabethan theatrical manager, made a reference in his diary to a performance of this play on June 11, 1594. Acting in it were members of the Lord Admiral's Men and of the Lord Chamberlain's Men, a group in which Shakespeare was an actor. Another Elizabethan, Thomas Lodge, referred to it in his *Wits Miserie, and the Worlds Madness*.

History relates that this *Ur-Hamlet* included dramatic elements like the ghost, the play-within-the-play and the duel, just as Shakespeare's *Hamlet* did. Further, Laertes and Fortinbras were characters in this version.

Earlier, Kyd had written *The Spanish Tragedy*, a prototype of the Senecan tradition then popular on the Elizabethan stage. In that play are elements of the same vengeful ghost, the protagonist's determination to seek vengeance and his emotional imbalance. Kyd's play was also characterized by an ingenious plot, clearcut motivation and rising suspense.

But the original story of Hamlet, one in which revenge is the dominant theme, can trace its roots back to the early middle ages in Northern Europe. We first hear about Hamlet's story in the *Historia Danica* written by Saxo Grammaticus, a Danish historian. Between 1180 and 1208 he put together a collection of true stories, legends and folk tales of Northern Europe. The story of Hamlet or Amlethus, as he was called, is found in the third and fourth books of Saxo's *His-*

toria. According to Saxo, Amlethus was a legendary hero from the tenth century who was locked for many years in a brutal struggle with his enemies. His father, Horwendil, Governor of Jutland, who was married to Gerutha, daughter of the King of Denmark, is openly slain by his brother Fergon who seizes the throne and marries Gerutha. Amlethus, a young boy at the time, grows up determined to avenge his father's murder.

Like Shakespeare's Hamlet, Amlethus feigns madness to deceive his suspicious uncle who devises several schemes to entrap him, all without success. His attempts include arranging for a woman to seduce him, hiding a courtier in his mother's room to kill him unawares, and sending him with two false friends to an intended death in England.

But Amlethus triumphs over these adversaries. He marries the English king's daughter, returns to Denmark and murders his enemies including his uncle. After ruling Denmark for several years, he marries a second Englishwoman who betrays him, and he is killed in battle by another uncle.

A second story of Hamlet was included in the fifth series of the *Histoires tragiques* written by Francois de Belleforest in 1576. In 1608, Thomas Pavier translated this version in England and called it *The Hystorie of Hamblet*. Belleforest's tale of revenge featured some differences from the original Saxo version. In Belleforest's story, Gerutha and Fergon commit adultery before Horwendil's murder, Hamlet is in love with the woman ordered to seduce him and he suffers from a melancholic disposition.

It can be concluded that although Elizabethan audiences were familiar with the Hamlet story, Shakespeare's version of a young man's brutal struggle to avenge his father's murder incorporated elements from the Saxo, Belleforest, and *Ur-Hamlet* versions of Amlethus, Prince of Denmark. Shakespeare turned the basic plot into superb theater not only by applying the conventions of Elizabethan drama, but also by showing the character development of a complex tragic hero in superior and timeless language.

Hamlet as Tragedy

Through the influence of certain plays of the Roman stoic philosopher Seneca (notably *Thyestes*), an important strand of drama developed in the late sixteenth century: revenge tragedy. Its popularity seems to have begun around 1589 with Thomas Kyd's *The Spanish Tragedy* and to have continued until 1641 with James Shirley's *The Cardinal*. Its ingredients were a son who sought revenge for some wrong (death, deposition) done to his father, a ghost who incited the revenge, a hero who reproached himself for some inability and adopted a pose of madness, crimes of adultery, incest, or murder, intrigue and counterintrigue, and devices such as witches and cemetery scenes. All these conventions, with the exception of witches, are found in some form in *Hamlet*. Nonetheless *Hamlet* is subject to interpretation as "pure tragedy" because the revenge motif is not unquestionably set forth to Hamlet and it does not explain the full conflict which he feels within him.

There are many ways of defining tragedy and thus many tragic elements that may appear in a literary work. Perhaps the simplest definition requires that the protagonist die at the end. However, to make his death significant enough for drama, it was felt that the protagonist should be of noble or important position, for others would then be affected directly by his death. Notions of tragedy developed in the Renaissance from Boccaccio's *De Casibus Illustrum Virorum* (Concerning the Fall of Noble Men), through John Lydgate's *The Fall of Princes*. Aristotle's discussion of tragedy was also influential. Hamlet's fall from the noble courtier, described by Ophelia, results in his death and the deaths of Polonius, Rosencrantz, Guildenstern, Ophelia, the queen, Laertes and the king. The people of Denmark have also suffered because of what happens to Hamlet and the ruling nobility of Denmark.

Another element which *The Fall of Princes* introduced into the tragic formulas of the Renaissance was that the fall should arise from the shortcoming within the prince: pride, perhaps, or an error of judgment. This idea coincides with Aristotle's statements concerning *hamartia* (popularly known as a tragic flaw, but better translated as an excess of some quality which becomes harmful). The tragic hero was dominated by this weakness and was thus responsible for his own misfortune and death, either through action or through inaction. The conflict of the play could arise from the hero's external relationships because of his *hamaria* or from internal struggles to overcome it, or from both.

The most discussed question about *Hamlet* is just what is Hamlet's tragic flaw. There are those who believe it is his inability to act or to make up his mind; there are those who see it as an Oedipus complex or as a death wish. Is his reason submerged by excessive passion? Does he really become temporarily insane? The narrative presenting his story should raise *pathos* (great feeling, suffering) in the audience through their recognition of at least potential elements within themselves or others they know, and *catharsis* (a purging of that pathos) through pity and fear. The play objectifies these feelings and thus eliminates them, which is the psychological definition of catharsis. At the conclusion of the play there should be an uplifting of the spirit if catharsis has taken place. Perhaps, therefore, the sense of a tragic "flaw" in Hamlet that an audience receives is one involving uncertainty through not knowing what is truth, what course of action to take and what results will ensue upon the action taken.

A more profitable way of looking at *Hamlet* as a tragedy is to perceive the wasting of good (Hamlet) in the process of driving out evil (Claudius). The emphasis, however, is upon the character of evil, not of good. At the moment of tragic vision, the hero comes to recognize the nature of things fully and his relationship to them (as in Act III, Sc. 2); this is called *anagnorisis*. Action then occurs which will both reverse the course of the play and bring an end not fully expected or intended; this is called *peripeteia*. As Hamlet acknowledges Claudius' guilt, he resolves to act. But his actions bring ends unforeseen by him at this time: Polonius' death, Ophelia's death, his own death.

Such ironic results are the foundation of the tragic spirit; they cast a pessimistic gloom over the play until the paradox of good and evil is understood. Hamlet's act brings suffering but ultimately achieves learning (*mathemata*), to employ Kenneth Burke's expression of tragic vision.

Stage History

The role of Hamlet has been a prime target of many major actors, and thus the reason for revivals of the play. Richard Burbage, the leading tragedian of Shakespeare's company, played the role in a way which received much public acclaim, as attested by several elegies written on his death in 1619. During the Puritan Interregnum (when the theaters were closed) an abbreviated form, called a droll, was presented; "The Grave-makers," as it was titled, was built around the last act. With the return of the king, the stage revived.

During the Restoration (and carrying into the eighteenth century), most of Shakespeare's plays were "improved" by omissions of unpleasant or allegedly unnecessary material, by additions of comedy or love affairs or music and dancing, and by reversals to happy endings. *Hamlet* endured less change than others; yet it was cut (both to get rid of "irrelevant" matter and to make it conform to usual length), scenes were transposed (supposedly to achieve unity and theatricality), and later a happy ending was added, with Hamlet living and Claudius dying. The most important actor interpreting the role in this period was Thomas Betterton (1635?-1710), the leading member of the Duke's Company.

The role of Hamlet was played by such eighteenth-century tragedians as Robert Wilks (1665?-1732); the great David Garrick (1717-1779), who adapted *Hamlet* at the Drury Lane in 1772 to make it one of his greatest successes; Spranger Barry (1719-1777); John Henderson (1747-1785); and John Kemble (1767-1823) and his brother Charles (1775-1854). A Jubilee, organized by Garrick, was held at Stratford-upon-Avon in September 1769, though weather conditions created problems and curtailed some planned activities. This was the first of the Shakespearean festivals held each year in many places throughout the world. Garrick transferred the Jubilee, including scenes from *Hamlet*, to the Drury Lane where it was repeated almost a hundred times. Around the turn of the century John Kemble attempted to restore Shakespeare's text and devised special and more historically accurate costumes, and thus we see the start of a return to study of the play as Shakespeare wrote it.

But in the early nineteenth century Shakespeare was more widely read than acted. Not until William Macready (1793-1873) began to produce the plays in elaborate staging and with full restoration of text (after 1837) was the public offered distinguished Shakespearean theater. Macready also acted the important roles. Charles Kean (1811-1868), like his father Edmund, dominated a production as "star" and carried Kemble's historical staging and costuming to often lampooned extremes. The next star was Henry Irving (1838-1905), the play being tailored to highlight his role. Yet here was also an artist concerned with the integrity of the entire performance, and his 1878 production of *Hamlet* accordingly stands out as a major theatrical accomplishment. Two more end-of-the-century giants must be mentioned: Johnston Forbes-Robertson (1853-1934), who produced *Hamlet* in 1897 with Mrs. Patrick Campbell (1865-1940), and Herbert Beerbohm Tree (1853-1917). Not all these versions, however, allowed the heroic ending we read to take place.

The role of Hamlet even attracted Sarah Bernhardt at the Théâtre Français in mid-century. Foreign productions (including those in America) during the eighteenth and nineteenth centuries were the result of the influence of traveling British troupes. The twentieth century has seen frequent revivals of the play. The way some people today read the play is largely conditioned by whom they saw act in it: John Barrymore (whose "O Vengeance" rang to the ceiling for a full minute), John Gielgud (reflective, intellectual, melancholic), Maurice Evans (a sort of breast-beating — or rather brow-beating — declamation with precise, but inaccurate, articulation), Donald Wolfit (a sympathetic view of a young man troubled by externals), Laurence Olivier (whose 1948 movie was played with obvious Freudian motifs and illogical cinematic settings), and Richard Burton (in a contemporary stage-rehearsal production by Gielgud, in which once in a while characters spoke in character). This latter version was presented in movie houses and perhaps has become the "standard" for today's generation.

Perhaps no Hamlet, character or play, is going to be satisfactory to all critics and public alike. Most seem to read the play, and thus the title role, in special ways. More than any other play it draws great actors and fiery disagreements. But if nothing else, and regardless of specific production, the viewing of the play as Shakespeare wrote it will impress the audience with its theatricality, its unity, its movement, its great poetry and even its comedy.

Plot Summary

A ghost, which looks like the late king of Denmark, has appeared to sentries at the castle of Elsinore, which is armed in case of attack from Fortinbras, prince of Norway. The sentries have brought Horatio, a friend of Hamlet's, to observe the ghost; it appears, disappears, reappears and finally leaves as the cock crows. Later in the day the king of Denmark, Claudius, brother to the late king who had defeated Fortinbras' father, sends messengers to the king of Norway (Fortinbras' uncle), gives Laertes (Polonius' son) permission to return to France and inquires about Hamlet's melancholic state. Hamlet's father, we learn, has been dead only two months, but his mother has married his uncle, who has now become king. Horatio informs Hamlet of the ghost; they arrange to meet that night to see whether it will appear.

At Polonius' house, Laertes advises his sister Ophelia not to trust Hamlet or be seduced by him. Then Polonius, an adviser to the king, says goodbye to Laertes, advising him to remain aloof from entanglements with his fellow man. Next he cautions Ophelia not to believe Hamlet and to report to him her contacts with the prince. That night the ghost appears again, beckoning Hamlet to a private talk. The ghost states that it is the spirit of Hamlet's father, who had been murdered by the present king. While he slept in his orchard, his brother Claudius poured poison in his ear. Hamlet is told to set things right, but to leave his mother's punishment to heaven.

Polonius sends Reynaldo to spy on Laertes in France and then questions Ophelia about an encounter with Hamlet. Polonius concludes that Hamlet's thwarted love has made him mad. The king commissions Rosencrantz and Guildenstern, friends of Hamlet, to find out what is troubling him. Fortinbras' successes are recounted, and Polonius advances his theory about Hamlet's disposition, giving as evidence a letter written to Ophelia. Hamlet enters and Polonius tries to get him to explain what is bothering him. Rosencrantz and Guildenstern next interview Hamlet, who is aware of their true purpose. The conversation turns to a traveling troupe of actors who have come to provide entertainment for the royal assemblage. After talk of plays and players, an actor recites lines about the death of Priam, king of Troy. Hamlet arranges for the actor to insert a playlet into the evening performance. He then regrets his inability to act upon his plan of revenge.

Further preparations are made to spy on Hamlet. The king, Polonius and Ophelia conceal themselves while Hamlet meditates on what course of action he should take. Suspicious of Ophelia, who is instructed to enter into conversation with him, Hamlet dismisses her to a nunnery. The king recognizes what is troubling Hamlet and therefore decides to send Hamlet to England. Soon the play is presented. Horatio is to observe the king's reaction to it, and Hamlet sits at

Ophelia's feet. There is a pantomime, followed by a play, both of which show a king being murdered as the ghost had declared Hamlet's father was. The king rises and rushes away. Rosencrantz and Guildenstern, and then Polonius, inform Hamlet that his mother wishes to speak to him in her sitting room. Again Polonius will spy and the queen is to try to get at the reason behind Hamlet's behavior. On his way there, Hamlet sees the king at prayer, but delays killing him, so that he won't be saved because of being in a state of grace. Hamlet does not hear the king state his lack of real repentance. Polonius has preceded Hamlet to the queen's room and hidden himself behind a tapestry. The queen scolds Hamlet for offending the king. He speaks roughly to her, she cries for help, Polonius joins her calls, and Hamlet, thinking he is the king, kills him with his sword. Again Hamlet reproaches his mother for her complicity in the murder. He speaks with the ghost, which is unseen and unheard by the queen. He accuses his mother further and reveals that he knows of the plan to send him to England to get rid of him.

The queen tells the king about her interview with Hamlet and his slaying of Polonius. Rosencrantz and Guildenstern are sent to find the body, but Hamlet, who knows its whereabouts, speaks in riddles to them and then to the king. Hamlet is informed officially that he is being sent to England, and we learn that he is to be killed there. In the next scene, Fortinbras passes through Denmark to win back a little patch of ground belonging to Poland. Hamlet, observing this exposure to death and danger "even for an eggshell," is strengthened into bloody resolution to avenge his father. Ophelia has gone mad and sings incoherently of love and death. The people are riotous because of Polonius' death and shout that Laertes shall be king. Laertes then enters, set on revenge; the king tries to calm, but not dissuade him. The sight of Ophelia adds to Laertes' grief. Meanwhile, we learn from a letter delivered to Horatio that Hamlet has escaped with the help of pirates who attacked their ship. The king has apparently explained to Laertes how his father came to be killed, and receiving Hamlet's letter stating that he has returned to Denmark alone, the king plots the death of Hamlet in a duel with Laertes. Laertes has previously acquired poison in which he will dip his sword to insure Hamlet's death. The king is to prepare a poisoned drink, which he will offer to Hamlet during the duel. The act ends with the queen's report of Ophelia's death by drowning.

The final act begins with the sardonic humor of two gravediggers preparing a grave for Ophelia. Hamlet and Horatio observe them and remark on the remains of the dead that are unearthed. A funeral procession enters. Laertes protests that more rites should be said, but the priest refuses because Ophelia's death was "doubtful." Laertes, unable to control his grief, leaps into the grave, and Hamlet, finally aware of who has died, also leaps in. Each protests stronger feelings of grief, and they fight until attendants part them. A little later, Hamlet relates what occurred during his trip to England. He discovered the plot to kill him and altered the orders so that Rosencrantz and Guildenstern would be killed. Osric appears to bring a challenge for Hamlet from Laertes. The duel follows, the foils and the wine having been prepared. Hamlet is urged to drink, but does not. The queen unwittingly drinks the poisoned wine, Laertes wounds Hamlet, the swords are exchanged in a scuffle and Hamlet wounds Laertes. The queen dies. Laertes falls and denounces the king, who is stabbed by Hamlet. Both the king and Laertes die. Hamlet tells Horatio to tell his story, recommending that Fortinbras be elected king, and then dies. Fortinbras enters with English ambassadors, who inform the assemblage that Rosencrantz and Guildenstern are dead. Fortinbras has Hamlet nobly carried from the scene.

Summaries and Commentaries by Act and Scene

ACT I • SCENE 1

Summary

The setting of the opening scene is the royal castle at Elsinore on the rocky sea-washed Danish coast. It is wintertime. The action begins when Bernardo, an officer, arrives on the platform of the castle rampart at midnight to relieve Francisco from his guard duty.

Francisco demands from Bernardo the night's password, "Long live the king." Presently, Horatio and Marcellus join Bernardo and identify themselves to Francisco as loyal subjects. When Francisco leaves, Bernardo tells Marcellus that the ghost has not appeared yet. Then Marcellus explains to Bernardo that Horatio has joined their watch to verify his theory that the ghost is a hallucination.

Just as Bernardo starts to describe the ghost's previous visits, it appears. Bernardo notes that the specter is dressed in armor and seems to look like the late king of Denmark. But when Horatio questions the ghost it disappears, and leaves the men astonished at what they have seen. Horatio then tells the others that the armor worn by the ghost is the same worn by King Hamlet when he defeated the Poles and fought against Fortinbras, the elderly king of Norway.

Horatio also informs the others that military preparations are taking place at Elsinore because young Fortinbras of Norway, the present king's nephew, seeks to reclaim the Norwegian lands his late father lost to King Hamlet. For this purpose, young Fortinbras has raised an army from the rabble willing to fight for minimal wages.

Horatio then compares the appearance of the ghost to the ominous events that occurred in Rome before the assassination of Julius Caesar. Suddenly the ghost reappears. When Horatio commands the specter to speak, it fades away just as the cock crows. The scene ends with Horatio telling the others that Hamlet must be informed of the ghost's appearance.

Commentary

In this scene, which begins the action of the main plot, Shakespeare evokes a mood of foreboding and mystery. The winter's night is dark and bitterly cold. Francisco ends his watch thankfully because he is "sick at heart."

The focus of the scene is the ghost whose appearance mystifies Horatio, Marcellus and Bernardo. Is it real? Although the ghost resembles the late king of Denmark, it could be a demon. But if it is really the late king's spirit, why has it come back from the dead? "A mote it is to trouble the mind's eye," says Horatio about the ghost, and likens its appearance to the ominous events in ancient Rome before the murder of Julius Caesar.

The appearance of the wordless ghost is an important dramatic device that Shakespeare uses to stir a number of questions in our minds as well as to rivet our attention on the action.

In Elizabethan times, ghosts were objects of great mystery. The prevailing theory was that ghosts were unsettled souls returned from the grave to complete unfinished business. On the other hand, a ghost could be a demon, Satan's messenger. At this point, Horatio and his friends fear the ghost may be a demon.

Horatio, we learn, is a scholar and trusted by Marcellus and Bernardo. He serves as a reliable witness to the ghost's appearance and as conveyor of this news to his good friend Hamlet. He also reports that Denmark is preparing to deal with the military threat led by young Fortinbras, nephew of the old and senile king of Norway. Horatio's speech touches on retribution and honor, two themes which are central to the play.

ACT I • SCENE 2

Summary

A trumpet fanfare signals the grand entrance of Claudius, Gertrude, Hamlet and some courtiers into a stateroom. There will be a special audience to end official court mourning for the late King Hamlet who has been dead only two months.

When Claudius and Gertrude are seated, Claudius informs the court that even though the king has been dead only a short while, Claudius and Gertrude, the king's widow, were married for the good of the state. He thanks the court for their support in electing him to the throne and in his marriage to Gertrude. He reports that Prince Fortinbras of Norway has been preparing for war against Denmark to recover Norwegian lands won by the late King Hamlet. To put an end to these threats, Claudius reports that he has asked his envoys, Cornelius and Voltemand, to deliver letters that he has written to Fortinbras' elderly uncle, the king of Norway.

Then Claudius turns to Laertes to hear his petition to return to France. Claudius says he knows how dear Denmark is to Laertes' father, Polonius, who supported him in his election to the throne. Since Polonius has already given Laertes permission, although reluctantly, to return to France, Claudius gives his.

Claudius turns to Hamlet who is wearing mourning clothes and asks him why he looks so downcast. Gertrude, Hamlet's mother, beseeches Hamlet to stop his mourning for his father saying all that lives must eventually come to an end. Hamlet replies that these outward trappings of grief do not do justice to his inner feelings. Claudius tries to reason with Hamlet by saying that all mourning must come to a reasonable end and that to prolong mourning is unnatural. He asks Hamlet to think of him now as a father because Hamlet is his heir to the Danish throne. The king and queen urge Hamlet to remain in Denmark instead of returning to school in Wittenberg. When Hamlet agrees to stay, Claudius invites the court to celebrate Hamlet's decision.

Alone, Hamlet describes his inner thoughts in his first soliloquy. He reveals that he wishes he could disappear from the earth. He rails against the sudden death of his father and calls his mother's swift marriage to his uncle incestuous. Using bitter language, he compares the virtues of his father with the faults of his uncle and accuses his mother of unfaithfulness to his father's memory.

Horatio, Marcellus and Bernardo arrive on the scene and interrupt Hamlet who is especially pleased to see Horatio, an old friend. When Horatio tells Hamlet that he came from Wittenberg to attend King Hamlet's funeral, Hamlet bitterly comments that the same food was served at the funeral as at the wedding.

Horatio then tells Hamlet that they have seen a ghost on the castle rampart that looks like Hamlet's father. After Horatio describes the ghost's appearance, the shocked Hamlet agrees to join the watch that night. When his friends leave, Hamlet admits in a soliloquy that he suspects some foul play.

Commentary

This scene introduces us to King Claudius, the antagonist. In his first speech, we learn that Claudius is a man of decisive action. His sudden marriage to Gertrude, "our sometimes sister, now our queen,/ Th' imperial jointress . . ." was an act of patriotism, he says, to ensure the safety of Denmark. Claudius also shows decisive action in dealing with the aggressive behavior of Prince Fortinbras of Norway.

He is reasonable but critical of his nephew Hamlet's continued mourning of his father's death, which he calls "obstinate condolement." His criticism of Hamlet's behaviour implies that it is unbefitting of an heir to the Danish throne.

Claudius' call for celebration when Hamlet agrees to stay in Elsinore reveals that Claudius wants to forget the past and end the old order in a suitable fashion.

Queen Gertrude, by her new husband's side, reveals her maternal feelings towards Hamlet in urging him to cease his mournful ways. But her hasty marriage has incurred her son's displeasure.

Polonius, lord chamberlain, is a powerful ally of the new king. His description of his son's petition as "laboursome" is ironic in light of Polonius's later drawn-out speeches. His well-mannered son, Laertes, we discover, prefers to live in France away from the court.

The significance of this scene is that we meet Hamlet, the protagonist, and learn about his troubled mind. Although Hamlet mourns his father's sudden death, we glean from his asides and his soliloquy that the source of his depression is his mother's hasty marriage to his uncle, the newly elected king of Denmark.

It should be pointed out that marriage between a man and his dead brother's wife was considered incestuous and so, when Gertrude and Claudius married, their action violated canon law. But it is interesting that their subjects support the marriage incestuous or not.

It is also important to realize that a throne is not necessarily passed to the eldest son. Both in Norway and Denmark, a brother rather than a son has become king through election. We should not feel that Hamlet has been denied a throne that was rightfully his. The similarity between Hamlet's and Fortinbras' situation should be noted.

While the young idealistic Hamlet condemns his mother and step-father for tarnishing the image of the Danish royal family, we discover that Hamlet also clearly dislikes Claudius as a person. When his uncle calls him "my cousin Hamlet, and my son," Hamlet replies with the play on words, "A little more than kin, and less than kind!" He does not feel kindly disposed to his uncle and says "I am too much i' the sun."

From Hamlet's more direct response to his mother's words, we learn that his mourning clothes and grieving demeanor are but a poor reflection of his inner despair. In this passage between Hamlet and the queen, Shakespeare develops his appearance versus reality theme. To the queen's question "Why seems it (his father's death) so particular with thee?" Hamlet replies, "Seems, madam? Nay it is. I know not 'seems.'" He then explains that the grief he bears goes beyond the "trappings and the suits of woe."

It must be noted that the soliloquy was an important dramatic device which allowed a character to reveal his innermost thoughts and feelings aloud. These revelations help the audience understand the motivations behind the character's actions as the play unfolds.

In Hamlet's first soliloquy, he reveals that his despair has driven him to thoughts of suicide and that he would kill himself if self-murder were not a violation of canon law. Further, we learn that his father's death and his mother's hasty remarriage have turned his world into "an unweeded garden/That grows to seed; things rank and gross in nature/Possess it merely." He demonstrates his knowledge of Greek mythology when he calls his father Hyperion, the sun god, in contrast to his stepfather whom he calls a satyr, and also when he condemns his mother's drastic change in behavior from weeping widow "like Niobe, all tears" to incestuous bride. Unfortunately, Hamlet leaps from the single example of his mother's impulsive behavior and condemns all women for all time with the comment, "Frailty, thy name is woman!"

His dialogue with Horatio reveals Hamlet's deep affection for his friend. His sardonic words to Horatio, "The funeral bak'd meats/Did coldly furnish forth the marriage tables," tells Horatio about Hamlet's feelings toward the hasty marriage of his mother and uncle.

At the end of the scene Horatio describes the mysterious appearances of the armored ghost to an anxious Hamlet. The use of short questions and answers ("Pale or red?/Nay, very pale") increases the tempo and spurs Hamlet into action. He says "all is not well" and suspects "foul play."

ACT I • SCENE 3

Summary

The scene opens in the house of the lord chamberlain, Polonius. Laertes, his son, is ready to set sail for France. He tells his sister Ophelia that his possessions are on the ship, bids her farewell and asks her to write him letters. But he takes the time to caution her not to take Hamlet's attentions seriously because his royal birth means that he must choose a wife carefully. He advises Ophelia to protect her virtue at all costs. Ophelia agrees to follow her brother's advice but suggests that he follow it too.

When Polonius enters, he chides Laertes for still being there, but gives him his blessing and then lectures him on a gentleman's code of behavior. He advises Laertes to keep his thoughts to himself, act wisely and with self-control, cherish old friends and choose new ones wisely and to stay away from quarrels, but if in a fight give a good account of himself. He instructs Laertes to listen to others but keep his own counsel, select his wardrobe with care because a man's clothes reveal the man underneath, never lend or borrow money and, finally, to be true to himself.

When Laertes departs, Polonius questions Ophelia on her relationship with Hamlet. He pokes fun at her foolishness in thinking that Hamlet is sincere in his attentions toward her. Finally, he orders her to end her relationship with Hamlet because no good will come of it.

Commentary

This scene provides an insight into Polonius' family life and introduces the reader to another element of the plot, the romance between Hamlet and Ophelia.

In his lengthy speech on womanly conduct, Laertes reveals a patronizing attitude towards his sister. He is certainly unsympathetic to her relationship with Hamlet, and he credits her with little common sense. Polonius echoes this advice in his lecture to Ophelia. Further, he actually forbids her to see Hamlet again. These two, in fact, do Ophelia a great disservice. Both Laertes and Polonius reject the notion that Hamlet could be serious in his intentions towards Ophelia. First Laertes says:

His greatness weigh'd, his will is not his own;
For he himself is subject to his birth.
He may not, as unvalued persons do,
Carve for himself, for on his choice depends
The safety and health of this whole state,

(Act I, Sc. 3, 17-21)

Then Polonius pokes fun at Ophelia, and ends with this advice:

        In few, Ophelia,
Do not believe his vows; for they are brokers;
Not of that dye which their investments show,
But mere implorators of unholy suits,
Breathing like sanctified and pious bawds,
The better to beguile.

(Act I, Sc. 3, 126-31)

The other significant speech in this scene is Polonius' advice to his son on man-of-the-world conduct. The speech reveals Polonius' long-winded style, but more important, it reveals the superficial nature of the man's character — one who is more interested in his public image. However, the speech is memorable for its last lines that, although ironic, suggest a deeper thoughtfulness.

This above all — to thine own self be true,
And it must follow, as the night the day,
Thou canst not then be false to any man.

(Act I, Sc. 3, 78-80)

ACT I • SCENE 4

Summary

Hamlet, Horatio and Marcellus are on the castle rampart at midnight waiting for the ghost to appear. Hamlet explains that the noise they hear in the background is only the king drinking and celebrating the festive season. Hamlet then criticizes this behavior as unseemly because it has given Denmark a bad reputation for drunkenness and obscures Denmark's finer achievements. Further, he likens a nation's weakness to a flaw in a man's character which he says a man can inherit, nurture or develop. This flaw can poison a man's good qualities.

The ghost suddenly appears. Hamlet excitedly asks the apparition whether it is a good spirit or a wicked goblin, and why it has come. The ghost beckons Hamlet to follow it, but the others fear that the ghost will harm Hamlet. They try to restrain him. Hamlet scoffs at their fears and continues to follow the ghost off stage, saying that it his fate that leads him on. The others follow him.

Commentary

The action of the main plot is accelerated when Hamlet meets the ghost.

Since Elizabethans believed that ghosts could be evil spirits, Hamlet, Horatio and Marcellus' fear of the ghost is quite appropriate. But the fact that the ghost resembles Hamlet's late father causes Hamlet to identify him as the late king and to exclaim, "Say, why is this? wherefore? What should we do?"

The sense of foreboding is heightened when Hamlet follows the ghost like his destiny. He says, "My fate cries out/And makes each petty attire in this body/As hardy as the Nemean lions nerve." Marcellus' line "Something is rotten in the state of Denmark," underlines this sense of foreboding.

Hamlet's criticism of the revelry in the background earlier in the scene must be noted. The king's carousing inside the castle serves as a sharp contrast to the serious business on the battlements.

But Hamlet's famous "dram of evil" speech (14-38) is not a mere lecture on how one flaw in a man's character can corrupt the whole man and bring about his downfall. It serves as an explanation for Hamlet's future behavior and therefore is full of irony.

Hamlet offers three reasons why a flaw may be present in a person. The first, "As in their birth, — wherein they are not guilty,/Since nature cannot choose his origin, —" absolves the person of any responsibility for his behavior. He is a victim of fate. The third reason, "Or by some habit that too much o'erleavens/The form of plausive manners," tells us that men can develop bad habits that will bring about their downfall. But it is the second source of corruption — "By the o'ergrowth of some complexion/Oft breaking down the pales and forts of reason," — that speaks of Elizabethan theories on human behavior.

A man's "complexion" refers to his temperament which is determined by the four bodily fluids called humors. Since the humors were blood, phlegm, red bile and black bile, a person could have a sanguine, phlegmatic, choleric, or melancholic personality depending on which humor was in excess. Further, Elizabethans believed that intellectual types like Hamlet were susceptible to melancholy or excessive brooding that blocked their ability to act constructively.

ACT I • SCENE 5

Summary

The ghost identifies himself to Hamlet as his father's spirit forced to wander by night and to suffer purgatorial fires by day until his sins have been forgiven. He urges Hamlet to avenge his murder, "a murder most foul." He says that although his sudden death was blamed on a serpent sting, he in fact was murdered by Claudius, "that incestuous, that adulterate beast."

With passion, the ghost tells Hamlet that his uncle Claudius poured poison into the king's ears as he lay sleeping in the orchard. Because he was murdered, he died without sacraments to absolve him of his sins. As a result, he is condemned to wander the earth from dusk to dawn until his sins are forgiven and he gains admittance to heaven. But while he asks Hamlet to avenge his murder, he warns Hamlet to spare his mother because her guilt and heaven will punish her.

When the ghost leaves, Hamlet in an emotional soliloquy says that the ghost's call for revenge has wiped out everything else in his mind.

Horatio and Marcellus come upon an overwrought Hamlet who recovers a little and makes his friends swear to keep secret what they have seen. Although Horatio and Marcellus are puzzled by Hamlet's words and erratic behavior, they do as he wishes. The ghost's sepulchral voice is heard in the background.

Hamlet adds a further oath. If he feigns madness, his friends are not to take notice of any bizarre behavior. Hamlet thanks his friends and curses the enormity of the task that lies ahead.

Commentary

This scene clearly belongs to the tragic tale of the unshriven ghost. In his vulnerable state, Hamlet readily accepts the ghost as his father's spirit and agrees to avenge his murder even before he hears the details.

> Haste me to know't, that I, with wings as swift
> As meditation or the thoughts of love,
> May sweep to my revenge.
>
> (Act I, Sc. 5, 29-31)

There is even a slight suggestion that Claudius may have seduced Queen Gertrude before King Hamlet's death: "O wicked wit and gifts,/that have the power/So to seduce! —" The ghost also refers to Claudius as an "adulterate beast."

Then to his horror, Hamlet learns the true story of his father's death: "Cut off even in the blossoms of my sin,/. . . sent to my account/With all my imperfections on my head." Now to Hamlet's initial concern — the sudden marriage of Claudius and Gertrude — is added the revenge of his father's murder. But it is significant that this revenge excludes his mother.

> Taint not thy mind, nor let thy soul contrive
> Against thy mother aught. Leave her to heaven,
> And to those thorns that in her bosom lodge
> To prick and sting her.
>
> (Act I, Sc. 5, 85-88)

30

Throughout the scene, the ghost's anguished speeches heighten the dramatic effects. Even when the ghost is out of sight, his tortured voice still echoes Hamlet's injunction to his friends to take an oath of secrecy at what they have seen, although, significantly, Hamlet keeps the ghost's story to himself.

Hamlet realizes what an enormous burden he has to bear. When the ghost says "Let not the royal bed of Denmark be/A couch for luxury and damned incest," it looks as though Hamlet must not only avenge his father's death to redeem his own honor but also perform a public service. Now the play's important theme of honor and revenge has been clearly launched.

ACT II • SCENE 1

Summary

In this scene, the action returns to the house of Polonius. He is in the midst of instructing his messenger, Reynaldo, on how to make inquiries of Laertes, who is in Paris, without his knowledge. Polonius tells Reynaldo that first he should locate other Danes in Paris who would know Laertes and identify himself as a friend of the family. Then he should elicit information by suggesting a few of the activities in which young-men-about-town indulge. Although Reynaldo thinks this scheme may dishonor Laertes, Polonius explains that this indirect method is best.

When Reynaldo leaves, Ophelia enters in a distressed state. She reports to her father that she has been frightened by the sudden appearance in her room of a disheveled Hamlet. Her description of his behavior causes Polonius to think that Hamlet is mad with love-sickness because Ophelia has rejected his attentions. Polonius says the king must know of Hamlet's behavior in order to prevent further problems.

Commentary

This scene provides an interlude in the action of the main plot. We find out more about Polonius' meddlesome character. Although his underhanded methods of finding out about Laertes' behavior in Paris stop short of dishonoring him ("and there put on him/What forgeries you please; marry, none so rank/As may dishonour him — take heed of that;"), they reveal an unsavory side of Polonius' character which prepares the reader for his later behavior. It would appear that while Polonius says "And let him ply his music," he is more concerned that Laertes not ruin his father's reputation at court.

Ophelia's report to her father of Hamlet's shocking demeanor tells us that Hamlet has put into action his plan of feigning madness:

And with a look so piteous in purport
As if he had been loosed out of hell
To speak of horrors — he comes before me.

(Act II, Sc. 1, 81-83)

Why Hamlet chose Ophelia to appear to as "pale as his shirt, his knees knocking each other," is open to dispute. The important point is that this action advances and links plot elements with the main plot. For it is Polonius who will report Hamlet's "very ecstasy of love" to the king who must be told of Hamlet's behavior.

Polonius seems sincerely sorry, "I am sorry/What, have you given him any words of late?" and his closing speech is tinged with pity:

> Come, go we to the King.
> This must be known; which, being kept close, might move
> More grief to hide than hate to utter love.
>
> (Act II, Sc. 1, 117-19)

But his chief concern is not for his daughter for, while as the king's adviser he must report the prince's unusual behavior, Polonius is also eager to demonstrate his own wisdom and insight.

ACT II • SCENE 2

Summary

The king greets Rosencrantz and Guildenstern who have been summoned to court. Claudius explains his concern over Hamlet's bizarre behavior. Because of their early friendship with Hamlet, Claudius has chosen these two to find out if Hamlet is troubled with other concerns besides his father's death. The queen also welcomes Rosencrantz and Guildenstern and adds that she is confident that their mission will be helpful and much appreciated by the court.

The two young men both agree to do their best in their service to the king. Their majesties thank them and they leave to find Hamlet. Polonius enters and announces the return of Cornelius and Voltemand, the two ambassadors sent to Norway. When Claudius praises Polonius as the bearer of good news, Polonius blurts out that he has found the cause of Hamlet's strange behavior. Although Claudius asks him to speak of that, Polonius suggests that the king first admit the ambassadors.

Voltemand reports to Claudius that the king of Norway has put a stop to his nephew Fortinbras' plans to invade Denmark. Instead, he has given Fortinbras money and allowed him to raise an army to invade Poland, and has asked that Fortinbras be given permission to march across Danish territory enroute. Claudius declares his pleasure with the report, but will reply to the Norwegian king's request once he has studied the situation.

Polonius now begins discussing Hamlet but with such a wordy introduction that the queen suggests he get to the point. He states that Hamlet is indeed mad and reads a letter he has written to Ophelia. Polonius says that this letter, a mixture of bad prose and verse, proves Hamlet's infatuation for Ophelia. Therefore, Polonius claims, the source and cause of Hamlet's lunacy must be unrequited love. He then urges the king and queen to believe him because his conclusions have proven correct in the past, but he says he will obtain additional proof. His plan is to let Ophelia and Hamlet meet while he and the king are hidden behind a curtain to observe their encounter.

Polonius hurries everybody out of the room so that he can question the prince. In the ensuing exchange of words, Hamlet talks in riddles to Polonius, advises him to safeguard his daughter's virtues and finally ridicules him. But Polonius interprets Hamlet's odd behavior as positive proof that he is in fact suffering love-sickness. He rushes off to arrange an encounter between the two lovers just as Rosencrantz and Guildenstern arrive.

Hamlet greets the two men as "excellent good friends" and joins with them in harmless banter until he suspects what they have been sent for. After he forces them to admit the real purpose of their visit, he tells them to report to their majesties that all joy has gone out of his life, and that he has lost interest in the world, in men and even in women. Rosencrantz replies that the prince will not then enjoy the performance of the players whom they passed on their way to Elsinore.

But Hamlet shows an interest in "he that plays the king." Further questioning tells Hamlet that they are the "tragedians of the city" who have been forced to travel because a company of child actors has become popular and has usurped the players' position. The prince again welcomes Rosencrantz and Guildenstern to Elsinore but adds that he is not as mad as their majesties believe.

At that moment, Polonius enters and announces the arrival of the actors. Once again, Hamlet resumes his mad behavior and mocks Polonius, who is unaware that he is being ridiculed. When four or five players from the company enter, Hamlet greets them, reminding them of their past meetings, and asks them for a "passionate speech." He requests Aeneas' tale to Dido from Virgil's *Aeneid*.

After the first player recites in epic style the slaying of King Priam by Pyrrhus, son of Achilles, Hamlet asks Polonius to look after the players' living quarters. He then turns to the first player and arranges with him for the company to perform the play *The Murder of Gonzago*. Sixteen lines are to be added to the script by Hamlet.

Once the players leave him, Hamlet rails against himself that a player could express such impassioned grief in a drama yet he, Hamlet, cannot act against Claudius on his real-life grief. Once he denounces himself for being a coward and a villain, he realizes that this anger is a pointless emotion and that he must get on with his task.

Then he outlines his plan to have the players perform *The Murder of Gonzago* before the king and court. During the play, he will observe his uncle's expression for any flinching that would indicate guilt. Hamlet justifies his action by saying he needs substantial proof that his father was murdered by his uncle because the ghost may have been a devil who assumed a "pleasing shape" to lead the prince to damnation.

Commentary

The significance of this scene is that the main characters make plans to entrap each other and in doing so, reveal their true nature and intentions. To begin with, Claudius is suspicious of Hamlet's antic behavior and so summons Rosencrantz and Guildenstern, two of Hamlet's childhood friends, to court. He instructs them to find out the cause of Hamlet's strange actions. Thus he says:

> . . . so by your companies
> To draw him on to pleasures, and to gather
> So much as from occasion you may glean,
> Whether aught to us unknown afflicts him thus
> That, open'd, lies within our remedy.
>
> (Act II, Sc. 2, 14-18)

The queen, on the other hand, does not wish to entrap Hamlet, but because she sincerely wants her son's well-being restored, she goes along with the king's plan.

Rosencrantz and Guildenstern are typical courtiers who serve their king with loyalty and without question. Shakespeare makes them identical in character, manners and language. They are unaware of the king's underlying motive. When Hamlet greets them warmly later in the scene Shakespeare records their friendly banter in prose rather than in verse. This change in style is a dramatic device used to denote a lowering of pitch in the action. Prose is often used in light or comic sections.

But after Hamlet engages in witty small talk with his two old friends about the whimsies of "fortune," he realizes that there is more to their visit than appears. After forcing them to reveal the real purpose of their visit, he tells them to inform their majesties that he has "lost all my mirth, forgone all custom of exercises." Further, he now views the universe as "a sterile promontory" and a "foul and pestilent congregation of vapours" while he says "man delights not me — nor woman neither."

While Hamlet in his disillusionment no longer feels at home in the world, he assures his two friends that "my uncle-father and aunt-mother are deceiv'd," because he is not as mad as they think. But he doesn't tell them anything more.

Voltemand and Cornelius' return to court tells us that several weeks have passed since Hamlet first saw and spoke to the ghost. Their report tells us that Fortinbras, who like Hamlet has lost a father, has clearly given up the idea of fighting Denmark and instead has chosen to invade Poland. Fortinbras' decisive action contrasts Hamlet's growing inaction.

Polonius also is suspicious of Hamlet's behavior. He launches into a tedious explanation of Hamlet's antic behavior that shows Polonius to be wordy, pompous and overly confident. Although he says "brevity is the soul of wit,/And tediousness the limbs and outward flourishes," his discourse on the mystery of Hamlet's behavior is stretched out with exercises on words, such as day, night, time and others. As he does not follow his own advice, his speech provides comic relief in the mounting tragedy.

The infamous letter written by Hamlet to Ophelia contains an odd selection of prose and verse which even Polonius takes delight in criticizing. Because it is a poor effort, it is possible that Hamlet purposely wrote it to find its way into Polonius' hands as additional evidence of Hamlet's madness. But Polonius insists that the prince's madness has been caused by Ophelia's rejecting his love. Although he admits that he ordered Ophelia to spurn Hamlet's advances, he now gets agreement from the king for his plan to verify the reason for Hamlet's madness. With no sensitivity for his daughter's feelings, he says, "At such a time I'll loose my daughter to him./Be you and I behind an arras then."

The subsequent discussion between Polonius and Hamlet is significant because he continues to establish his antic behavior by mocking Polonius, a man for whom Hamlet would ordinarily show the greatest respect because of his age and his high court position. Hamlet's sudden question to Polonius "Have you a daughter?" and his warning "Let her not walk i' th' sun. Conception is a blessing, but/As your daughter may conceive — friend, look to't," are full of irony. He could be cautioning Polonius to keep Ophelia out of court intrigue, but the warning falls flat on Polonius. He is more than ever convinced that love-sickness is the reason behind Hamlet's behavior. Hamlet's other veiled warning to Polonius, "O Jephthah, judge of Israel, what a treasure hadst thou!" also misses the mark. However, the sequence affords more comic relief before the rising action.

The arrival of the players enables Hamlet to make a plan for entrapping Claudius. But before the prince arranges the performance of *The Murder of Gonzago* with his addition of 16 lines, it is significant that he asks one player to deliver a stirring rendition of an act of vengeance from ancient Greece. In that story, the avenger Pyrrhus suffered a momentary delay in killing Priam but recovered himself and went on to avenge his father, Achilles.

> And never did the Cyclops' hammers fall
> On Mars's armour, forg'd for proof eterne,
> With less remorse than Pyrrhus' bleeding sword
> Now falls on Priam.
>
> (Act II, Sc. 2, 477-80)

In his soliloquy, Hamlet is moved to denounce himself for his inaction and cowardice in contrast to the decisive action of the hero of the Greek drama.

Yet I,
A dull and muddy-mettled rascal, peak
Like John-a-dreams, unpregnant of my cause,
And can say nothing!

(Act II, Sc. 2, 551-54)

When Hamlet's passion abates, he swiftly reveals a plan for entrapping Claudius, "to catch the conscience of the king," and to establish his guilt. His method is not that of the heroic Achilles but more in keeping with Hamlet's scholarly character.

The rhyming couplet, a typical Shakespearean device, signals the end of this act and whets our appetite for future intrigue.

ACT III • SCENE 1

Summary

When this scene opens, Rosencrantz and Guildenstern are reporting their findings on Hamlet's behavior to the king. Hamlet has confessed to them that he feels "distracted" but will not speak of the cause. When Gertrude questions them, they reply that Hamlet received them cordially and seemed pleased to hear that players had arrived. Polonius, who is also present, adds that Hamlet would like their majesties to watch a performance of a play.

The king agrees to see the performance, and shows delight in Hamlet's new interest which he urges Rosencrantz and Guildenstern to encourage. They leave. Claudius then asks Gertrude to leave so that Polonius can put into effect his plan for Ophelia and Hamlet to meet. Claudius and Polonius will hide behind a curtain to eavesdrop on their conversation.

Polonius directs Ophelia to read a book of devotions while she waits for Hamlet. In an aside Claudius reveals his "deed" as a "heavy burden." The two men withdraw just before Hamlet enters.

In his third soliloquy, Hamlet reflects on the notion of suicide as a means of escape from life's problems. He concludes that the fear of the unknown after death keeps us all living. He then notices Ophelia who says she wants to return some gifts that he gave her. Hamlet denies that he ever gave her anything. To her surprise, Hamlet questions her honesty and fairness and then contradicts himself by saying that "I did love you once," and then, "I loved you not." Then Hamlet tells her to get to a "nunnery" because men cannot be trusted. They are "arrant knaves all."

Abruptly, he inquires where her father is. To her reply that he is at home, he retorts that home is the best place for a fool. By this time,

Ophelia is quite distraught but Hamlet continues his verbal abuse of marriage and womanhood. When he finally leaves, Ophelia declares her deep sorrow over Hamlet's apparent breakdown.

The king and Polonius join Ophelia. The king declares that Hamlet doesn't sound like a man in love, more like someone suffering from an affliction of the soul. Since he sees Hamlet's behavior as a threat, he decides to send him to England, a country whose ruler owes Denmark tribute.

Although Polonius still thinks that Hamlet is suffering from lovesickness, he agrees with the king's decision. He tells his daughter Ophelia that they heard everything, so she need not say anything. He makes one request of the king, that he let the queen discuss firmly with her son his melancholy while Polonius listens from a hiding place. If the queen fails to find out his secret, then let Claudius send him to England, or elsewhere. Claudius agrees.

Commentary

As the scene begins, the king is most anxious to discover from Rosencrantz and Guildenstern the reason for Hamlet's "confusion,/ Grating so harshly all the days of quiet/With turbulent and dangerous lunacy." But he still presents his solicitous stepfather appearance when he accepts Hamlet's invitation to see a performance of the play.

Claudius' aside where he reveals the reason for his fearfulness is noteworthy because it prepares us for his reaction to *The Murder of Gonzago.* We have the first indication that his outwardly calm behavior is concealing a tormented conscience when Claudius says:

How smart a lash that speech doth give my conscience!
The harlot's cheek, beautified with plast'ring art,
Is not more ugly to the thing that helps it
Than is my deed to my most painted word.
O heavy burden!

(Act III, Sc. 1, 50-54)

Gertrude still presents herself as Claudius' devoted wife and Hamlet's concerned mother. She is the one who asks Rosencrantz and Guildenstern if they have interested Hamlet in a pastime that would divert his melancholy.

When everyone leaves, the stage is set for Hamlet's most well-known soliloquy, "To be, or not to be — that is the question." The questions he ponders in this soliloquy are those with which every man or woman wrestles in times of great crisis. When Hamlet asks "Whether 'tis nobler in the mind to suffer," he is wondering whether it is better to respond passively to the trials and tribulations of life; or is it better to take action and confront problems. — "and by opposing end them;" or is it best to commit suicide: "to say we end/The heartache, and the thousand natural shocks/That flesh is heir to." But Hamlet points out that the problem with suicide is man's fear of oblivion:

> But that the dread of something after death —
> The undiscover'd country, from whose bourn
> No traveller returns — puzzles the will,
> And makes us rather bear those ills we have
> Than fly to others that we know not of?
>
> (Act III, Sc. 1, 78-82)

The above passage is also significant because it seems to say that ghosts are excluded from other "travellers" who do not return from the unknown. Perhaps Hamlet means that human beings do not return in the form of flesh and blood but only in spirit. How else can you explain the appearance of his father's ghost which is so central to the play's action?

The position of this soliloquy in the action has puzzled critics over the years. The main problem seems to be that it reveals the same Hamlet we met in Act I in his first soliloquy. At that time he contemplated death because he was so devastated by his mother's marriage to his uncle. Now he contemplates suicide as an easy solution to all life's conflicts. At the end of Act II, Hamlet seemed to be a man of action, rational, and determined to carry out a plan that would expose his uncle's duplicity. Now he reverts to the procrastinating prince. He is surely subjected to many mood changes — perhaps typical of his melancholic personality. Whatever the reason, he is caught in the vise of a monumental conflict and he continues to struggle for a satisfactory solution.

In his subsequent encounter with Ophelia, we witness the behavior of a devastatingly cruel Hamlet, even though he feigns madness. One should believe that his behavior is predicated on knowing that he has been set up. It is Hamlet's bitterness, then, that lashes out at Ophelia when he denies that he ever loved her, orders her to a nunnery and calls all men "arrant knaves, believe none of us."

But his attacks on womanhood must not be ignored. They have probably been precipitated by his mother's marriage, which he calls incestuous, and by his awareness that Ophelia, like Rosencrantz and Guildenstern, has been recruited by the king to spy on him. Although his description of the perfidy of women (142-149) probably drew laughter from Elizabethan audiences, it illustrates Hamlet's continued attack on womanhood and his obsession with marriage.

What is more important is that Ophelia is now convinced of Hamlet's madness. Her speech that begins with the memorable line, "O, what a noble mind is here o'erthrown!" reveals her remorse over her lost love, the paragon of Renaissance manhood.

But Claudius questions the theory that Hamlet is suffering from love-sickness. The symptoms don't fit. Now Polonius has another scheme to force Hamlet's real problem into the open and if that fails, he will be sent to England. As Claudius says, "It shall be so./Madness in great ones must not unwatch'd go."

ACT III • SCENE 2

Summary

Hamlet enters with three of the players and instructs them on how to deliver the lines of *The Murder Of Gonzago*. He also discusses the techniques of acting and warns them against exaggeration of an action. Polonius arrives with Rosencrantz and Guildenstern to announce that their majesties are ready to "hear this piece of work."

Hamlet praises Horatio for his steady temperament that does not give into passion, and then shares the details of *The Murder of Gonzago* with him. He requests Horatio to observe his uncle's reaction to one particular speech. If he doesn't react in a guilty fashion as Hamlet anticipates, then Hamlet says both have seen a ghost, but not King Hamlet's spirit. Horatio agrees to help.

While the court is assembling, Hamlet resumes his lunatic demeanor and engages in banter with Claudius and Polonius. He refuses to sit beside his mother and reclines at Ophelia's feet to engage in some bawdy repartee.

The pantomime before the play shows a loving king and queen together. When the king falls asleep on a bank of flowers, she leaves. A man enters, takes off the king's crown and kisses it, pours poison in the king's ears and leaves him. The queen returns, finds the king dead and expresses her grief. The murderer returns with some henchmen and the dead body is removed. The murderer then woos the queen who at first resists his attentions but in the end accepts his love.

To Ophelia's questions, Hamlet replies that the actor who speaks the lines of the prologue will explain the action. Then the player-king and player-queen enact *The Murder of Gonzago*. In the dialogue, the player-queen declares that she will not remarry if widowed. As the player-king falls asleep, Hamlet asks the queen how she likes the play. Gertrude replies that the player-queen protests too much. Then Hamlet, in reply to Claudius' question, calls the play "The Mousetrap."

When Lucianus, the player-king's nephew, enters, Hamlet's excitement begins to grow, and he urges the actor playing the role of the murderer to get on with his speech. As the murderer pours the poison into the player-king's ear, Hamlet tells the audience that the king's name is Gonzago, that the story is true and that soon they will see how Lucianus wins Gonzago's wife.

Claudius suddenly rises and cries out for light while Polonius calls for an end to the play. Hamlet, alone with Horatio, is ecstatic with the effect of his play and declares he now believes the ghost's story. Horatio agrees that Claudius reacted to the play.

Rosencrantz and Guildenstern return to inform Hamlet that the king is indisposed, and the queen wants to have a private talk with her son. The messengers ask Hamlet once more "the cause of his distemper." He replies that it is thwarted political ambition, but they do not understand. Polonius enters with the same message from the queen and Hamlet again pretends to be mad and talks in riddles.

When the others leave, Hamlet's soliloquy reveals bloodthirsty and murderous thoughts. With much effort, he restrains his anger because he doesn't want to inflict physical harm on his mother when he meets with her.

Commentary

It is important to note that in this scene Hamlet's behavior runs the gamut of emotions. When the scene opens, we see him as a rational intellectual. But as the action develops and the climax is reached in the play-within-the-play we witness his emotions gradually controlling his reason as he becomes excessively excited and then murderously angry.

In the first episode, Shakespeare uses Hamlet to voice his opinions on the art of acting. As a playwright and actor himself, Shakespeare had first-hand experience between histrionics and eloquence (17-22). In this episode we see a rational Hamlet discussing the techniques of acting with authority and as one who enjoys the theater. He is quite a different Hamlet from the embittered abusive prince who verbally attacked Ophelia. This passage serves to relax the tension of the previous scene.

Hamlet's instructions to the players also indicate that he is concerned they will present a performance in their play that will achieve the desired result of touching Claudius' conscience.

Hamlet's praise of Horatio is significant because he considers him a perfect and well-balanced man.

> For thou hast been
> As one, in suff'ring all, that suffers nothing;
> A man that Fortune's buffets and rewards
> Hast ta'en with equal thanks;
>
> (Act III, Sc. II, 63-66)

Hamlet admires a man whose temperament is properly balanced between passion and reason, "blood and judgement." He shows his trust in Horatio by asking him to observe Claudius. The lines:

> If his occulted guilt

Do not itself unkennel in one speech,
It is a damned ghost that we have seen,
(Act III, Sc. 2, 78-80)

reveals that the ghost's story will be vindicated, and Hamlet will accept the outcome.

Once the court is assembled, Hamlet resumes his strange behavior: "I must be idle." His whimsical reply to his uncle's inquiries that reveal he is suffering from frustrated ambition are meant to conceal his true motives, just as his use of puns with Polonius and bawdy language with Ophelia reveal more disrespectful behavior. But his bitter comment to Ophelia on how quickly a man's memory disappears in time prompts him to say that man needs to build a monument to himself lest he be forgotten (126-129).

The pantomime that precedes *The Murder of Gonzago* has puzzled many critics. The chief reason for Hamlet's including the dumb show is probably so that the court and the audience will fully understand the action in Gonzago's murder. But it also serves to prime the pump of Claudius' guilt.

When Lucianus pours the poison in Gonzago's ear, Claudius reacts with alarm and rushes off. The jig is up. This episode marks the climax of the play, for the peak of the rising action is reached when Hamlet establishes Claudius' guilt. Now Claudius knows that Hamlet is clearly his adversary and poses a threat to his security as King of Denmark and Gertrude's husband. But for the moment, Hamlet is ecstatic.

O good Horatio, I'll take the ghost's word for a thousand
    pound!
Didst perceive?
(Act III, Sc. 2, 274-75)

When Rosencrantz and Guildenstern inform Hamlet that Claudius is indisposed, he is still in a mood of elation. But these two pasteboard courtiers are impatient with his antic behavior. Nevertheless, Hamlet assures them with irony that he still loves them, "by these pickers and stealers!" Then he shows his further contempt of these two in the passage:

'Sblood, do you think I am easier to be play'd on
than a pipe? Call me what instrument you will, though
you can fret me, you cannot play upon me.
(Act III, Sc. 2, 353-55)

When Polonius enters, he is mocked again by Hamlet who continues his act of mental instability. However, when the others leave, the prince comments on the setting as "the very witching time of night," and reveals his bloodthirsty and murderous mood in the language of witchcraft. He is in the mood to seek revenge but restrains himself. When he sees his mother, he wants her to be aware of his anger, but he will refrain from physically harming her.

ACT III • SCENE 3

Summary

Claudius tells Rosencrantz and Guildenstern that since Hamlet's madness has become a threat, they are commissioned to take him to England as soon as possible. Rosencrantz and Guildenstern express their desire to help the king and declare that the welfare of the state depends upon the well-being of the king. Before they leave, they assure the king that they will act quickly. Polonius enters to report that Hamlet is going to his mother's bedroom and that he himself will hide behind a tapestry to overhear their conversation. Claudius thanks Polonius who then leaves.

Alone, Claudius curses his murderous deed. He compares it to Cain's murder of his brother Abel and wonders if he will ever be forgiven for this horrendous crime. Then he realizes that a repentant sinner is forgiven, but still he wonders if he can be forgiven as long as he retains his "crown, his ambition; and his queen." He realizes that heavenly justice is different from the earthly kind which tends to be corrupt. That being the case, he wonders what hope he has of being forgiven. He hopes that prayer will help.

Hamlet, with drawn sword, comes upon Claudius but doesn't murder him because he is at prayer. Hamlet declares that Claudius should die in a state of sin because Hamlet's father was murdered before his sins could be forgiven. He determines that hell will be the destination of his uncle's soul. When Hamlet leaves for his mother's room, the king rises saying that while his words are heavenward, his thoughts will never be.

Commentary

Claudius, the threatened antagonist, has begun to take action to rid himself and Denmark of Hamlet. His plan to send Hamlet to England is set into action and the faithful Rosencrantz and Guildenstern will carry out the king's orders with haste. In his soliloquy, Claudius reveals that he is tormented by a guilty conscience and agonizes over murdering his brother. "It has the primal eldest curse upon't,/A brother's murder!" he laments. As remorseful as he feels, Claudius is not prepared to give up his throne or his queen to redeem himself. Motivated by intense ambition, he has committed a mortal sin that will continue to torment his soul and influence his subsequent actions.

When Hamlet finds the kneeling Claudius, his overpowering hatred for the man almost provokes him to run him through with his sword. But because he wants his uncle to suffer the eternal damnation of hell, he will not carry out his revenge when Claudius is at prayer.

Some critics argue that Hamlet's decision to delay his revenge is an example of the procrastination that plagued him. However, to kill Claudius now would make for an unsatisfactory ending of the play, and force Hamlet to do something not within his character.

But it is important to note that Hamlet still behaves in the same ugly and angry mood of the previous scene as he makes his way to his mother's room.

ACT III • SCENE 4

Summary

Polonius instructs Gertrude to be firm with the prince when she confronts him with his antic behavior, and then hides behind the tapestry before Hamlet enters.

Gertrude begins to chastise her son, but his harsh replies frighten her and she cries for help. From behind the tapestry, Polonius hears Gertrude's voice and echoes her calls for help. Hamlet draws his sword, thrusts it through the tapestry and kills Polonius.

Hamlet thinks at first that he has killed the king. When his mother denounces the murder, Hamlet replies that it is almost as bad "as kill a king, and marry with his brother." To Gertrude's question of why Hamlet is so nasty to her, Hamlet replies that it is her marriage to Claudius that upsets him.

He points to two contrasting portraits, one of King Hamlet whom he describes in warm terms, and the other of Claudius whom he belittles. He wants to know how she could have married such a man, and then he accuses her of lusting for Claudius. Gertrude beseeches Hamlet to say no more, because his words make her feel remorseful. Suddenly the ghost appears to Hamlet who thinks it has come to remind him of his promise of revenge. But it expresses concern for Gertrude who now thinks her son is completely mad. When she asks what he is staring at, Hamlet becomes frustrated because his mother cannot see the ghost.

When the ghost leaves, Gertrude declares that what Hamlet saw was really a hallucination. The prince denies that he is mad and urges his mother to repent her guilty behavior. He urges her to stop sharing his uncle's bed and to not succumb to his lust.

Hamlet expresses his regret at Polonius' death and then bids his mother goodnight. Even though Hamlet sarcastically advises Gertrude to tell the king that Hamlet is "mad in craft" and "not in madness," she promises to keep their conversation secret.

Hamlet then informs his mother that he is being sent to England with Rosencrantz and Guildenstern whom he distrusts. He fears that the sealed letters they will carry are meant to seal his own fate, but he will outwit them. He states that he will remove the remains of Polonius, now so quiet, into another room and again says goodnight to Gertrude.

Commentary

In this scene, Hamlet's anger rapidly reaches full throttle in unfolding action that witnesses his passion overcoming his reason. He charges into his mother's room and angrily declares, "You go not until I set you up a glass/Where you may see the inmost part of you." But Gertrude's sudden fear precipitates a cry for help, echoed by the hidden Polonius who reveals his presence. Hamlet then vents his uncontrollable anger by thrusting his sword into Polonius.

We cannot quarrel with Hamlet's assessment of the scheming Polonius ("Thou wretched, rash, intruding fool, farewell!"), but we feel sorry for the elderly lord chamberlain because his excessive ambition to ingratiate himself with the king was his undoing. Even at the end of the scene, Hamlet shows his contempt for this busybody when he calls him "in life a foolish prating knave," and tells his mother, "I'll lug the guts into the neighbour room." It is not a dignified eulogy for the lord chamberlain of Denmark.

But it is Hamlet's relationship with the queen that warrants the most attention in this scene. Hamlet finally verbalizes his heartfelt thoughts of the hasty marriage between his mother and his uncle.

> Such an act
> That blurs the grace and blush of modesty;
> Calls virtue hypocrite; takes off the rose
> From the fair forehead of an innocent love,
> And sets a blister there; makes marriage vows
> As false as dicers' oaths.
>
> (Act III, Sc. 4, 40-45)

Hamlet cannot understand his mother's marriage to Claudius and accuses her of weakness and lust. He says: "You cannot call it love; for at your age/The heyday in the blood is tame, it's humble." His words denounce her lustful behavior and paint a portrait of a woman who is weak, sensual and not acting her age. More important, Hamlet's accusations find their mark. Although she had no reason to feel guilty about her remarriage, she now cries, "O speak to me no more!/These words like daggers enter in mine ears."

But Hamlet is not finished with his vile description of Claudius. While he compares the character of the late king to the four gods of the classical Pantheon, he calls Claudius, "a murderer and a villain," "a cutpurse of the empire and the rule," "a king of shreds and patches" and "a bloat king," which alludes to his drinking habits.

But his anger abates when the ghost suddenly reappears. The fact that the ghost appears for the last time at this point, and the fact that it appears only to Hamlet, has been cause for much critical speculation. From the ghost's own words we see that he not only reminds Hamlet of his promise but also prompts him to help his mother in her dilemma:

> Do not forget. This visitation
> Is but to whet thy almost blunted purpose.
> But look, amazement on thy mother sits.
> O, step between her and her fighting soul!
> Conceit in weakest bodies strongest works.
> Speak to her, Hamlet.
>
> (Act III, Sc. 4, 110-15)

Even the startled Hamlet thinks the ghost appears to reprove him for his inaction, "Do you not come your tardy son to chide." While some critics think it strange that the ghost appeared only to Hamlet, others think its appearance is a reflection of Hamlet's emotionally charged state of mind. In any case, having the queen see the ghost at this point would have interfered with the structure of the play and the motivations of the characters. Gertrude must remain innocent of her late husband's death and guilty only of lustful passion and poor judgment.

Other critics have offered several reasons for Hamlet's obsession with his mother's immoral behavior. The neo-Freudians interpret Hamlet's condemnation of his mother's behavior as a manifestation of an Oedipus complex (a son's unconscious lust for his mother). Others perceive Hamlet's behavior as in keeping with his moral idealism. At any rate, Hamlet advises his mother to refrain from further lovemaking with his uncle to redeem herself and lessen her guilt.

Nevertheless, although Gertrude thinks that Hamlet is mad, she will still prove her loyalty to her son and keep their disturbing discussion from the king "even for a pair of reechy kisses."

By the end of the scene, Hamlet's ironic comment, "Thus bad begins, and worse remains behind," makes us wonder about the consequences of Polonius' death. His final words lead us to believe that his erstwhile childhood friends, Rosencrantz and Guildenstern, are in for a few surprises.

ACT IV • SCENE 1

Summary
The king notices that Gertrude is upset and asks where her son is. After she dismisses Rosencrantz and Guildenstern, she reports to Claudius that Hamlet has gone mad and killed Polonius. The king

denounces the murder, but realizes that he would have been Hamlet's victim if he had been there. He wonders how he can explain Polonius' death to his subjects, and questions why he and Gertrude didn't restrain Hamlet earlier. He replies to his own question that it was their love for Hamlet that obscured their judgment.

Gertrude tells Claudius that the prince is now removing the body of Polonius, and that he regrets his murderous action. The king vows to send Hamlet away, and beckons Guildenstern who enters with Rosencrantz. Claudius tells them what Hamlet has done and asks them to find him and bring Polonius' body into the chapel. When they have left, Claudius explains to Gertrude that they must inform their wisest friends of their plans to avoid being blamed for Polonius' death.

Commentary

This scene prompts Claudius into ridding his court of Hamlet. He realizes that he was Hamlet's intended victim, "it had been so with us, had we been there," but maintains his loving uncle image by saying, "But so much was our love/We would not understand what was most fit." Nevertheless, Claudius can remove Hamlet from the court now without too many questions being asked.

Gertrude is clearly upset with Hamlet's behavior. Whether she keeps his secret or not, she informs Claudius that Hamlet is, "mad as the sea and wind when both contend/Which is the mightier." How else could Hamlet kill in cold blood "the unseen good old man."

ACT IV • SCENE 2

Summary
Rosencrantz and Guildenstern meet up with Hamlet who refuses to tell them where he has placed Polonius' body, but he agrees to go with them to see the king.

Commentary
Hamlet's strange behavior in this brief scene does not befit that of a tragic hero. Perhaps his actions are solely prompted by his contempt for the king's spies, Rosencrantz and Guildenstern. He compares them to a sponge "that soaks up the king's countenance (money), his rewards, and his authorities." But Hamlet warns these two that, "when he (the king) needs what you have glean'd, it is but squeezing you and, sponge, you shall be dry again."

ACT IV • SCENE 3

Summary
The king informs some members of the court that he has sent for Hamlet and for Polonius' body. He admits how difficult it is to con-

fine Hamlet because he is loved by all the people. Sending him into exile must appear to be the result of careful deliberation to avoid offending his subjects.

Rosencrantz enters to report that Hamlet will not reveal the whereabouts of Polonius' body. Guildenstern brings in the prince who replies to the king's questions with insolent remarks. Finally, he tells the king that Polonius' body may be found near the stairs leading to the lobby.

The king then informs Hamlet that he must be sent to England. Hamlet replies with more insolent remarks and then leaves. Claudius instructs Rosencrantz and Guildenstern to put him on board the ship to set sail that night. Alone, Claudius reveals that as soon as Hamlet arrives in England, he is to be put to death. Then Claudius will find peace at last.

Commentary

The king is clearly in charge as he attempts to explain his decision to send Hamlet into exile. However, he fears the reaction of "the distracted multitude" who love Hamlet.

Claudius also demonstrates a great deal of patience with Hamlet who mocks him and baits him instead of revealing Polonius' whereabouts.

There is irony in Claudius' remark, "So is it, if thou knew'st our purposes," when Hamlet thinks it's a good idea for him to go to England. In his short soliloquy, Claudius reveals that his sealed letters contain orders for Hamlet to be put to death on his arrival in England. Claudius is evidently desperate to keep his throne and his queen.

But it is Hamlet's preoccupation with death that deserves our attention in this scene. He points out in graphic language that death is the great equalizer of men — emperors and beggars alike: "Your fat king and your lean beggar is but variable service — two dishes, but to one table." He has grown to believe that man is insignificant indeed. But actually he has stumbled on the regeneration of life theory or the food chain theory: it all depends on your point of view.

A man may fish with the worm that hath eat of a king,
and eat of the fish that hath fed of that worm.

(Act IV, Sc. 3, 27-28)

In his last speech to Claudius, Hamlet continues to feign madness and says, "Farewell, dear mother." In that passage he may once again be alluding to his father's death and the incestuous marriage: his two obsessions.

ACT IV • SCENE 4

Summary

Prince Fortinbras of Norway arrives with his army and dispatches a captain to request permission from Claudius to cross Denmark on his way to Poland. Hamlet, in the company of Rosencrantz and Guildenstern, comes upon the captain. After questioning him, Hamlet learns that the Norwegian soldiers led by Fortinbras are going to fight Poland for a "little patch of ground/That hath in it no profit but the name."

Hamlet asks his escort to continue while he stops to consider what he has just heard. In a soliloquy, he compares his own indecision with Fortinbras' positive action against the Poles. He claims that when honor is at stake, it is right to act. He vows that he will stop wasting time, and avenge his father's death at last.

Commentary

Once again we meet Fortinbras, Prince of Norway, whose life is also affected by the pursuit of revenge. But in Fortinbras' case, we see a man of decisive action. In the name of honor, Fortinbras has raised an army of "landless resolutes" to invade Poland and attack a garrison. He appears to have mastered his emotions over his own father's death and his actions are now based on reason.

Nevertheless, Hamlet comments that war is just an excuse, "This is th' imposthume of much wealth and peace,/That inward breaks, and shows no cause without/Why the man dies." But Hamlet perceives Fortinbras' decisive action as another reminder that he has delayed his own revenge. He says, "How all occasions do inform against me/And spur my dull revenge." He questions why he has lapsed into such lassitude.

> Now, whether it be
> Bestial oblivion, or some craven scruple
> Of thinking too precisely on th' event, —
> A thought which, quarter'd, hath but one part wisdom
> And ever three parts coward,
>
> (Act IV, Sc. 4, 39-43)

These lines seem to indicate a characteristic inability to act, and only to anticipate the action. Although he realizes that "I have the cause, and will, and strength, and means/To do't," until now he has done nothing.

Hamlet is overwhelmed by Fortinbras' large scale attack on Poland all in the name of honor. He says, "Rightly to be great/Is not to stir without great argument,/But greatly to find quarrel in a straw/When honour's at the stake." He reproaches himself for his own inaction when he sees Fortinbras prepared to sacrifice 20,000 men to satisfy his own need to seek revenge. Hamlet's final lines, "O, from this time forth,/My thoughts be bloody, or be nothing worth!" seem to suggest that Hamlet will finally avenge his father's death. Fortinbras' example has pushed him into action. No more will he dawdle, moralize or feign madness.

ACT IV • SCENE 5

Summary

A courtier informs the queen that Ophelia wishes to speak with her. When the queen refuses, the courtier explains that Ophelia talks about her father and speaks in disjointed sentences. Horatio interrupts to say that her speech and behavior may cause suspicion. Gertrude then allows her to come in. Ophelia enters and sings several verses of ballads about love and the seduction of a maiden, and then sings about death that refers specifically to her dead father. Claudius, who has joined the others in the middle of Ophelia's recital, tries to get her attention without success. Before Ophelia leaves, she muses over the irregular burial of her father.

The king asks Horatio to watch her closely and he leaves to fill this request. Claudius then blames Ophelia's mad behavior on her father's death, and comments on the state of affairs at court. First Polonius is slain; Hamlet has left the kingdom; the subjects are confused and suspicious because Polonius had been buried in haste and secrecy; and finally Laertes has returned in secret from France and is upset by the ugly rumors he has heard. Claudius is greatly disturbed.

Noise is heard, and Claudius calls for his guards. A messenger enters to report that Laertes and some followers who call him Claudius' successor have overcome his officers of the guard and broken into the castle. Laertes then enters but asks his followers to guard the door outside, and then orders Claudius to "give" him his father.

Claudius succeeds in calming down Laertes with diplomacy, and assuring him that he, Claudius, is not guilty of Polonius' death. At that moment, Ophelia enters in a distracted manner. At the sight of his sister's pathetic state, Laertes can hardly contain his emotion. Meanwhile, Ophelia skips about, singing her sad songs while offering herbs and flowers to those assembled in the room.

When Ophelia leaves, Claudius promises that if Laertes discovers that he has been involved with Polonius' death, he will give him his kingdom. If not, he will join with him in finding the reason for Polonius' death.

Commentary

Ophelia's madness has struck some critics as being odd or unnecessary, while others have agreed that her madness and subsequent death are appropriate to the events of the falling action. First of all, we see her as an innocent victim of an overbearing father's foolishness. He ordered her not to see Hamlet, and then ordered her to entrap Hamlet, who rudely rejected her. Now the father whom she feared but respected has been violently murdered, and she has no one.

The young maiden who lived in a confused state unable to develop or demonstrate any maturity cannot cope with the loss of her father. It is interesting that the subjects of her songs alternate between her father's death and the romance she was denied. The legend of the baker's daughter who became an owl illustrates the plight of daughters who are forbidden to grow up. The love song about St. Valentine's Day gives us an insight into the romantic rejection she has experienced.

Laertes is understandably upset by the sight of his beloved sister who has lost complete touch with reality. "O heat, dry up my brains!" he cries when he sees her. But probably one of the most touching episodes in the play is the one in which Ophelia distributes her herbs and flowers whether real or imaginary. It is fitting that she give her brother rosemary, a symbol of remembrance used at weddings and funerals, as well as pansies, a symbol for thoughts. Although Laertes displayed the attitude of a man-of-the-world for his sister's adulation, he never demonstrated any thought for her human needs.

Now Laertes returns at the head of a mob to avenge his father's death and to uphold the honor of the family. He is certainly a man of action in contrast to Hamlet. The fact that he has inspired a mob to accompany him to the castle indicates his emotional appeal. He shows leadership qualities of acting quickly to right a wrong.

> I dare damnation. To this point I stand,
> That both the worlds I give to negligence,
> Let come what comes; only I'll be reveng'd
> Most throughly for my father.
>
> (Act IV, Sc. 5, 131-34)

But Claudius saves the day in this scene. Although he is faced with many problems, "When sorrows come, they come not single spies,/But in battalions!" he says, he exercises his great diplomatic skill and courage to neutralize Laertes' anger. He urges Laertes to be reasonable in finding out the true nature of his father's death. Claudius declares that if he is found to be guilty of Polonius' death, "we will our kingdom give,/Our crown, our life, and all that we call ours,/To you in satisfaction." To the end of this scene, Claudius is master of himself and the crisis. Only later do we discover the irony of his final words: "And we shall jointly labour with your soul/To give it due content."

ACT IV • SCENE 6

Summary

Horatio is told by his servant that some sailors wish to give him letters. Horatio asks the servant to let them enter and comments that Hamlet is the only person who could send him letters. The letter tells Horatio that the ship Hamlet was sailing on was attacked by pirates. In the ensuing fight, Hamlet boarded the pirate ship and was taken prisoner. He was treated well, and returned to Denmark on the condition that he do them a good turn. Horatio is to deliver the other letters to Claudius and then meet Hamlet without delay. Horatio asks the sailors to lead him to the prince.

Commentary

In this brief bridging scene, we hear about a quick-witted Hamlet who has managed to elude Rosencrantz and Guildenstern, and we wonder what happened to them. The sailors in the scene are probably those from the pirate ship who brought Hamlet back to Denmark. Now that all the major characters in the conflict are back in Denmark, we can anticipate a speedy resolution of the major action.

ACT IV • SCENE 7

Summary

The king has evidently told Laertes that Hamlet killed his father and even tried to kill Claudius. When Laertes asks the king why he failed to punish Hamlet for these crimes, Claudius replies that he had two reasons. First, the queen is devoted to her son, and since he is devoted to her, he restrained himself from taking action. The second reason is that the Danish people are very fond of Hamlet, and so Claudius could not expect their support of any punitive actions he might take against Hamlet. But Claudius assures Laertes that Hamlet will not escape without punishment.

A messenger enters with letters from Hamlet, one for the king and one for the queen. Claudius reads in his letter that Hamlet has returned to Denmark and will tell the king everything when they meet. Claudius is highly suspicious of Hamlet's return and formulates a plot with Laertes to murder Hamlet in an accident so that even his mother will not suspect anything.

Claudius explains to Laertes that Hamlet has been envious of Laertes' reputation as a skilled swordsman, and would like nothing better than to have a fencing match with him. The king points out to Laertes that he could avenge Polonius' death in such a fencing match. He adds that he will arrange a match between them, and that Laertes will use a foil with a sharpened tip. Laertes agrees with the plan and says he will dip his point into deadly poison to ensure Hamlet's death. Further, Claudius says he will provide a cup of poisoned wine for Hamlet to drink if by chance Laertes does not wound Hamlet in the duel.

Gertrude enters, and woefully informs Laertes that his sister has drowned. Gertrude explains that Ophelia was weaving garlands of flowers and hanging them on the limbs of a willow tree when she fell into the brook. Her spreading clothes kept her afloat for a while, until she sank to her death under the weight of them saturated with water.

Laertes is overcome with sorrow and leaves. Claudius tells Gertrude that he will have to soothe Laerte's rage once again.

Commentary

This scene prepares the stage for the final catastrophe. The cunning Claudius wastes no time in absolving himself of guilt in Polonius' murder and using his son, Laertes, in a plot to murder Hamlet.

But in the first episode of this scene, we see a king who truly loves his wife:

> She's so conjunctive to my life and soul
> That, as the star moves not but in his sphere,
> I could not but by her.
>
> > (Act IV, Sc. 7, 14-16)

Nevertheless, Claudius perceives Laertes's thirst for revenge for a "noble father lost," and a "sister driven into desp'rate terms," and so Hamlet's letter announcing his return prompts Claudius into villainous action with Laertes as a willing agent.

> And for his death no wind of blame shall breathe,
> But even his mother shall uncharge the practice
> And call it accident.
>
> > (Act IV, Sc. 7, 66-68)

First, he wins Laertes over to his scheme by flattery. He then approves of Laertes' plan to use a foil dipped in poison and then reveals that he will mix a poisoned drink himself to ensure Hamlet's death if all else fails. Poison was the most subtle and effective choice for killing because it was difficult to detect and it didn't make a mess, just as when Claudius used poison to murder King Hamlet.

But first, Claudius makes sure of Laertes' feelings towards his father's death. Says Claudius: "What would you undertake/To show yourself your father's son indeed/More than in words?" When Laertes exclaims, "To cut his throat i' th' church!" those violent words tell Claudius that he has a co-conspirator.

Laertes' behavior can be contrasted to Hamlet's. Hamlet has had over two months to avenge his father's death, but has procrastinated while he waits for the ideal moment. Laertes, on the other hand, is all action. Still, we have lost a certain amount of sympathy for Laertes. Even with a father murdered and buried without due ceremony, and a sister driven mad, we find his behavior questionable because he has chosen in his duel with Hamlet to use a sharpened and poisoned foil.

Hamlet, with his moral scruples and procrastination, emerges as a proper and tragic hero overwhelmed by evil. Yet again we empathize with Laertes in his sincere expression of grief for his drowned sister, Ophelia:

> Adieu, my lord.
> I have a speech of fire, that fain would blaze
> But that this folly drowns it.
>
> (Act IV, Sc. 7, 190-92)

The falling action is fast gathering momentum as one tragedy follows another. "One woe doth tread upon another's heel,/So fast they follow," says the queen before she announces tenderly the death of poor Ophelia. However, she makes it quite clear that Ophelia's death was accidental and not suicide because "an envious sliver broke," and she fell into the brook.

ACT V • SCENE 1

Summary

Two gravediggers enter and discuss the inquest into the death of Ophelia that was called to decide whether her death was accidental or suicide. One gravedigger remarks that she will have a Christian burial because she is a gentlewoman. While the other gravedigger goes to find a pitcher of liquor, Hamlet and Horatio enter. Hamlet is shocked to hear the gravedigger do his job with such lack of feeling as he digs and sings snippets of ballads. When he tosses up a skull, Hamlet comments on the fact that whatever a human being may have been in life, in his death he or she is just a collection of bones to toss around.

When the prince questions the gravedigger, his replies are so equivocal that Hamlet becomes impatient with his rudeness. The gravedigger finally tells Hamlet that he has been a sexton since the day when King Hamlet defeated old Fortinbras of Norway, the same day that young Hamlet was born.

Further questioning leads the gravedigger to pick up the skull that belonged to Yorick, the king's jester who died 23 years ago. Hamlet takes the skull and tells Horatio that Yorick was a childhood favorite who played countless games with him. Hamlet reflects that death brings the great and the small to this final state of grinning skulls.

Just then Ophelia's funeral procession arrives. Hamlet notices something irregular about the rites as he and Horatio hide themselves from view.

Laertes, Ophelia's brother, questions the priest on the modified funeral rites given his dead sister. The priest says that she is being given a funeral in keeping with her controversial death. Laertes then orders that Ophelia be lowered into the earth. The queen scatters flowers on her coffin lamenting the fact that she wanted her to be Hamlet's wife.

Unable to restrain himself any longer, Laertes leaps into the grave and begs to be buried with his sister. Hamlet then comes forward and leaps into the open grave with Laertes. The young man grabs the prince by the throat, and they grapple with each other until they are parted by attendants and climb out of the grave.

In his anger, Hamlet declares that he loved Ophelia more than Laertes could have loved her and mocks Laertes' pompous declaration of his sorrow. Then the queen declares that Hamlet is mad. Before Hamlet leaves, he demands to know why Laertes treats him this way when he has always liked him.

When Claudius is alone with Laertes, he reminds him of their scheme for vengeance.

Commentary

The first episode of this scene offers the kind of low comedy that was popular with Elizabethan audiences. But more important, the scene serves as comic relief before the subsequent tense action. The gravediggers, identified as two clowns, provide some broad comedy in prose as they discuss legal and theological questions in scholarly fashion.

While they inform the audience that there has been an inquest into Ophelia's death, they amuse us with their logical explanation of the outcome. "It must be se offendendo," says one clown instead of se defendendo, and continues to develop his argument with scholarly logic. The other clown discusses the finer points of accidental death versus suicide and also demonstrates his knowledge of Latin when he says "argal" instead of ergo. When one clown remarks that Ophelia will rate a Christian burial because she is a member of the aristocracy, the other clown is prompted to say that this is just another example of how the aristocracy have more rights than the common people. But then he points out that through Adam, the first delver or digger, they are descended from the first gentleman, and so their profession is an honorable one.

When Hamlet arrives on the scene, he is shocked to hear the insensitive remarks made by the gravedigger while he works. As he watches him, he ponders the bitter irony that ambitious politicians, toadying courtiers, vain court ladies, crafty lawyers and landowners still end up as the "quintessence of dust."

When Hamlet examines Yorick's skull, he is shocked at the brutal contrast between his good friend in life, full of laughter and fun that he knew so well, and the lifeless skull he holds in his hand. His reflections prompt him to think that even the great military generals and emperors, Alexander the Great and Julius Caesar, have ended up stopping "bungholes" with their remains. "O, that that earth which kept the world in awe/Should patch a wall t'expel the winter's flaw," he says in his disillusionment.

With the arrival of Ophelia's funeral procession, the mood changes from a preoccupation with death to the reality itself. We learn that the coroner had ruled Ophelia's death was suicide, but that the king has been able to intercede so she will be buried in sanctified ground. When Laertes complains about the "rites" to the priest, he is told that because Ophelia's death "was doubtful" she should really be buried in "unsanctified ground," and that "shards, flints, and pebbles should be thrown on her." Poor Ophelia! She gets poor treatment in death as well as in life. But the one respectful gesture is that she is allowed "virgin rites" because she died chaste, and so her mourners scatter flowers on her coffin.

Laertes' anguish over his sister's burial is particularly moving: "Lay her i' th' earth;/And from her fair and unpolluted flesh/May violets spring!" he says. We are again reminded of Ophelia's association with flowers, especially of the violet, symbol of faithfulness. The queen, who earlier reported that Ophelia's death was accidental, now laments, "I hop'd thou shouldst have been my Hamlet's wife," and we realize that both Polonius and Laertes were lacking in judgment to discourage marriage between her and Hamlet.

Hamlet's behavior in this scene deserves some comment. Because of his absence, we realize that he had no prior knowledge of Ophelia's madness or death, and so we understand his shock when he learns that he is witnessing Ophelia's funeral. Still, his authoritative behavior takes us by surprise when he announces himself, "This is I,/Hamlet, the Dane!" Then Hamlet's words to Laertes in this episode show him to be even more assertive, "For, though I am not splenitive and rash, /Yet have I in me something dangerous." His criticism of Laertes' melodramatic behavior emphasizes his continued dislike for histrionics. "I'll rant as well as thou," he says. Yet, Hamlet surprises us with his declaration that he loved Ophelia. "Forty thousand brothers/Could not (with all their quantity of love)/Make up my sum," he says.

However, there is irony in what Hamlet says, "That is Laertes,/A very noble youth. Mark." Once again things are not what they seem, and we know that the treachery Claudius has planned with Laertes will disprove Hamlet's unwary remark. With Claudius' final words, we are reminded that Ophelia's brother Laertes will seek his revenge and try to redeem his family's honor.

ACT V • SCENE 2

Summary

Hamlet and Horatio enter a hall in the castle. Hamlet is in the middle of telling Horatio his experiences since he left for England with

Rosencrantz and Guildenstern. Hamlet recalls that the first night at sea, he crept from his cabin and located the cabin of the two agents where he found the sealed packet containing Claudius' instructions to the English king. When he returned to his cabin, and opened the packet, he discovered that Claudius had ordered that Hamlet be beheaded in England. Acting quickly, he wrote new instructions requesting the English king to execute the agents who brought the commission. The prince folded up the instructions just as the original ones were folded, sealed them in the packet with the seal on his father's signet ring and returned them to the agents' quarters. The next day was the sea-fight with the pirates that Horatio had already known about. Hamlet was their only captive, and the others went on to England.

Horatio is astonished at Claudius' villainy. Hamlet asks Horatio if he thinks Hamlet now has just cause to kill Claudius considering his treachery. But Horatio warns Hamlet that Claudius will soon learn what has happened to his agents. Hamlet then confesses his regret for his angry outburst with Laertes earlier.

Osric, a courtier, enters and Hamlet recognizes him as one of the fashionable, well-mannered but affected men at court. In the subsequent dialogue, Hamlet teases Osric and mocks his mode of expression. Osric finally gets a chance to inform Hamlet that the king has arranged a friendly fencing match between Laertes and Hamlet that is to take place before the king and queen and their attendants. Hamlet agrees to the duel and says he will win for the king. When Osric leaves, Hamlet and Horatio comment on his foolishness. A lord enters to ask when Hamlet will be ready for the duel. He replies that he is ready when the king is and he is told that both the king and queen are coming to watch the match.

When the two friends are left alone, Horatio warns Hamlet that he will lose his wager, but Hamlet replies that he doesn't think so because he has been practising fencing since Laertes went to France. Horatio urges him to postpone the match if he has any suspicions, and adds that he will announce to the others that he is indisposed. But Hamlet explains that he is willing to accept his fate.

The king, queen, Laertes, Osric, lords and other attendants enter the room with foils and gauntlets. On a nearby table sit the flagons of wine. Before taking his seat, the king places Laertes' hand in Hamlet's. Hamlet expresses his regret for his anger towards Laertes earlier and asks Laertes to pardon his behavior stating that it was his madness that caused his outburst. Laertes replies that he's sure Hamlet meant no harm, but that he will not offer full pardon until the experts have assured him his name and honor are unblemished.

The king commands Osric to bring the foils, and then asks Hamlet if he knows the wager. Hamlet says he realizes that the king has wagered on the weaker side, but the king assures him that although

Laertes has improved since he went to France, the king has the odds. While Laertes chooses his foil, Hamlet inquires if all the foils are the same length. Then he chooses his. Before the match begins, the king orders that cannons be fired if Hamlet scores the first or second hit and announces that he will drink a cup of wine in his honor. Further, he will place a precious pearl in the cup to be drunk by the successful swordsman. After the sound of kettledrums, trumpets and cannon, the king drinks to Hamlet and the contest begins.

After Hamlet scores the first hit, Claudius calls for a drink of wine and urges Hamlet to join him to get the pearl he has won. But Hamlet refuses saying he wishes to continue. He achieves another hit which Laertes acknowledges. The king remarks to Gertrude that Hamlet will win but she says she doesn't think so because he's in poor condition. Then to the horror of the king, Gertrude picks up the cup of poisoned wine and drinks from it. She offers it to Hamlet who refuses to drink, and then offers to wipe his brow.

In an aside, Laertes assures the king that he will hit him now, but the king doesn't think so. To himself, Laertes admits a twinge of conscience. Hamlet urges him on to resume the match, and in their play Laertes wounds him. But in the confusion, they exchange rapiers and Hamlet wounds Laertes. Then the queen falls. Horatio shows concern for the bleeding Hamlet, and Osric shows concern for the wounded Laertes, who remarks that he is killed with his own treachery.

When Hamlet inquires after the queen, the king says she has only fainted at the sight of blood. But the queen revives a little to cry out that the wine she drank was poisoned. Hamlet orders the doors to be locked to detect the treachery in the court. Laertes tells Hamlet that they are both near death and that he holds the "treacherous instrument" in his hand. He adds that Gertrude has been poisoned and the king is to blame for all of it. Hamlet then turns swiftly to the king and strikes him with his sword, while he denounces him. The king then dies. Before Laertes dies, he asks Hamlet's pardon exclaiming that Hamlet is not to blame for Polonius' or Laertes' death nor is Laertes to be blamed for Hamlet's death.

Hamlet says that he is dying, and bids his dead mother farewell. He asks Horatio to report his story and his cause after his death. But Horatio wishes to join Hamlet in death. Hamlet stops him from drinking the poisoned wine saying that he has to survive to clear Hamlet's name.

When Hamlet inquires about the distant sound of cannonshot, Osric replies that young Fortinbras, on his victorious return from Poland, has fired a salute to the newly arrived English ambassadors. Just before Hamlet dies, he prophesies and approves the election of Fortinbras as King of Denmark. Horatio then pays Hamlet a moving tribute.

Fortinbras and the English ambassadors enter. The Norwegian

prince is shocked at the sight of so many dead bodies. The ambassadors agree that the spectacle is horrible, and add that they are too late to report to Claudius that Rosencrantz and Guildenstern have been executed as he requested.

Horatio asks Fortinbras to give orders to place the bodies on view and to let him report to the unknowing world how this tragedy came to pass. Fortinbras calls upon four captains to prepare Hamlet for military burial with the full honors that he deserves.

Commentary

Although this scene provides the final catastrophe of the action, the first episode concerns an exchange of information between Hamlet and Horatio about Hamlet's rescue from certain death, and serves to demonstrate Hamlet's change of behavior. From the start, we see a Hamlet who is decisive and clever in his actions, specifically in dealing with Rosencrantz and Guildenstern's commission. Although he says, "Sir, in my heart there was a kind of fighting/That would not let me sleep," he was able to save his life through rash action. But there is irony in his further statement, "There's a divinity that shapes our ends,/Rough-hew them how we will —." The fact that he sent his false friends Rosencrantz and Guildenstern to their death and even now feels no qualms of conscience about this deed ("They are not near my conscience; their defeat/Does by their own insinuation grow."), shows a change in attitude.

Further, he has come to terms with the whole matter of avenging his murdered father. Now his hatred is focused only on Claudius:

> He that hath kill'd my king, and whor'd my mother;
> Popp'd in between th' election and my hopes;
> Thrown out his angle for my proper life,
> And with such coz'nag — is't not perfect conscience
> To quit him with this arm?
>
> (Act V, Sc. 2, 64-67)

Still, Hamlet's courteousness shows when he regrets his earlier behavior toward Laertes, and he realizes that his thirst for revenge parallels his:

> But I am very sorry, good Horatio,
> That to Laertes I forgot myself;
> For by the image of my cause I see
> The portraiture of his.
>
> (Act V, Sc. 2, 75-78)

Before the final catastrophe, Shakespeare treats us to another bit of comedy in prose in the exchange between Osric and Hamlet. Here

Shakespeare is satirizing the overly affected manner and language of some English courtiers of the time. Hamlet mockingly calls Osric a waterfly who skims along the surface of life, and forces him to stop flailing the air with his hat: "Put your bonnet to his right use. 'Tis for the head." But Osric also serves to explain the rules of the fencing match to Hamlet.

As innocent as the fencing match sounds to Hamlet, Horatio has a sense of impending disaster about it and urges Hamlet to withdraw from the challenge. But even with his show of bravado, Hamlet says: "But thou wouldst not think how ill all's here about my heart. But it is no matter." The significance of this exchange is that although Hamlet senses danger, he seems to be prepared for his destiny. Even though there is no question that he is a skilled swordsman, he no longer fears death. He says, "Since no man knows aught of what he leaves, what is't to leave betimes? Let be."

Before the match begins, it is ironic that Hamlet apologizes for his rude behavior towards Laertes at his sister's funeral. Although he says, "His madness is poor Hamlet's enemy," he refers to the emotional extremes that have plagued him since the night his father's murder was revealed to him. But Laertes compounds the irony with his hypocritical statement of honor and revenge, "But till that time I do receive your offer'd love like love,/ And will not wrong it." We know that Laertes has a different concept of honor than Hamlet and that his mode of seeking revenge has already been set in motion.

At the start of the match, the king behaves more like an affable host than a Machiavellian villain. He calls for music and wine, but the treacherous schemer has poisoned the wine. He continues to press Hamlet to drink some between his palpable hits. Then Claudius loses confidence in Laertes' ability to wound Hamlet with his poisoned foil: "I do not think't," he remarks when Laertes says, "My lord, I'll hit him now."

The catastrophe when it comes happens rapidly. The queen collapses from the effects of the poisoned wine, the antagonist Claudius is killed by Hamlet, and then Laertes and Hamlet both die from being scratched with the poisoned foil. Ironically, it was poison that began the rottenness in Denmark and it is poison that has now claimed the lives of so many victims.

Laertes redeems himself by confessing to Hamlet Claudius' part in the treachery, saying, "The King, the King's to blame." Laertes also absolves Hamlet of all blame:

> Exchange forgiveness with me, noble Hamlet.
> Mine and my father's death come not upon thee,
> Nor thine on me!
>
> (Act V, Sc. 2, 315-17)

Hamlet finally redeems himself by confronting the king, "Here, thou incestuous, murd'rous damned Dane," lunging at him with his sword and killing him.

The noble Horatio, like the ancient Romans who committed suicide to be with their friends in death, wishes to die with Hamlet, but his purpose is clearly to stay behind to report this tragedy to the world and to Fortinbras. Says Hamlet:

If thou didst ever hold me in thy heart,
Absent thee from felicity awhile,
And in this harsh world draw thy breath in pain,
To tell my story.

(Act V, Sc. 2, 332-34)

It is significant that Fortinbras, Prince of Norway, should return from his Polish conquest at this time to fill the vacant Danish throne and carry on the affairs of state.

Hamlet, the tragic hero, will have a military funeral with all the honors. At last he is at peace:

Now cracks a noble heart. Good night, sweet prince,
And flights of angels sing thee to thy rest.

(Act V, Sc. 2, 345-47)

Finally, Horatio will recount to Fortinbras and others Hamlet's tragic story of man's struggle with the doctrine of revenge and his conflicting perceptions of truth and reality.

And let me speak to th' yet unknowing world
How these things came about. So shall you hear
Of carnal, bloody, and unnatural acts;
Of accidental judgments, casual slaughters;
Of deaths put on by cunning and forc'd cause;
And, in this upshot, purposes mistook
Fall'n on th' inventors' heads.

(Act V, Sc. 2, 365-71)

Characters

Methods of Analyzing Characters

1. Describing the Characters

It is always a good idea to begin any commentary on characters with a brief description of each of them—what they are like, what they seem to think about themselves, etc. This kind of brief survey of the characters assures the student that he will not assume too much when discussing the characters in more complex or sophisticated ways. It also forces the student not to overlook any of the various characters' essential attributes. It should be pointed out that Hamlet is the young prince of Denmark, or that Othello is a Moor; then these simple facts should be amplified by whatever else we know. All in all, then, one should make a short survey of the characteristics—both emotional and physical—of the characters.

2. Analysis of Character Development

Probably the most important aspect of character analysis is the treatment of the development of the characters, and primarily the main characters. It is all-important to explain how a character *changes* in the course of the play. And one must also explain *why* those changes take place *when* they do. Even if a character seems static throughout, there must be an explanation. It may be that Shakespeare is using the character as a prop, a necessary convenience, or simply as an illustrative example of an alternative to the mode of existence courted by the hero or heroine. When certain emotions—such as greed, hate, love, revenge, bitterness, confidence—come to the surface, we should try to understand precisely how and why. Is there violent reaction or calm acceptance? Does Lady Macbeth's incipient guilt plunge her into a quasi-psychotic depression? The basic changes, not the minor ones, should be briefly delineated and more thoroughly analyzed. Is it right that a certain character feels as he does? Is it human or is it extreme? Abnormal or normal? Unusual or typical? Surprising or expected? Are changes foreshadowed? Are they ever illogical or too contrived? All literary analysis consists of an extended process of asking questions. And this questioning process is particularly vital to the analysis of characters. We must understand why characters behave and change in order to understand the meaning of the entire play. Aside from all the usual reasons that characters change, as, for example, when one's mother or relative is killed and one suddenly is filled with a desire for revenge and acts accordingly, many explanations of character change can be found either in their motivation, as it is developed by the dramatist, or by the demands of the themes. And these will be our next two considerations.

3. Motivation

In considering the motivation of characters we are fundamentally enlarging our answer to the "why" of character behavior. Shakespeare is of course very "modern" in his grasp of human psychology and the ways in which thought should be translated into action. What incites Hamlet's anger at the beginning of the play is his sense of the immorality and haste of his mother's marriage to his uncle so soon after the death of his father. Later, after his encounter with the ghost, Hamlet has an even greater claim to outrage. After learning that his uncle has murdered his father, Hamlet's actions become motivated by revenge. While revenge is the force that drives Hamlet, it is self-preservation that motivates Claudius in his actions. To conceal his guilt and maintain both his kingdom and his queen are Claudius' prime concerns. There are explanations for the behavior of all the characters in the play, and these explanations or motivations must be considered by analyzing who and what they are.

4. Thematic Characters

Often we discover that the behavior of certain characters can be explained by themes. That is, a character like Iago may act in evil ways consistently because allegorically he represents evil. The play is about the destruction wrought by evil and thus Iago may be said to be a "thematic character," less human and less complicated, while more conventional and "stock." Any character in any play may be thought of as a thematic character from one point of view or another, but we generally limit our use of the term to characters who clearly represent certain dominant abstractions which are clashing in a play—i.e., good and evil, love and hatred, loyalty and disloyalty, faithfulness and unfaithfulness (notice how all are extensions of good and evil). Most tragedies involve thematic characters, but not in such ways that we choose to discuss the characters in those terms. In general, it is better to search for what is human or unique about certain characters, but it is always worthwhile to mention briefly the thematic possibilities of the characters. Why are they in the play? Why do they behave as they do? How does their behavior demonstrate particular ideas?

5. Analyzing Character Relationships

Although inherent in the other methods, the analysis of the relationships between the characters can be used as a complete analysis in itself. The world of the play is largely defined by the nature of the different relationships. Hamlet's relationships with the other characters in the play reveal different aspects of his personality and the personalities of those with whom he is in contact. The "more" or the "less" of the basic relationships of friendship, marriage, command, etc., must be clarified, for through this clarification of relationships, we arrive at a greater understanding of the characters themselves.

Character Sketches

Hamlet

Hamlet is the prince of Denmark, son of the late King Hamlet and Queen Gertrude, and nephew of Claudius. He is a young man of physical valor and scholarly preoccupations, and a student at the University of Wittenberg. He has returned home to find his father dead and his mother married to his uncle. He is in a distracted state of mourning, and even more significantly perhaps, of grief over his mother's quick remarriage. His father's ghost appears, tells of his murder at the hand of Claudius, and urges Hamlet to avenge both the foul play and the "incestuous" marriage.

Many penetrating and scholarly studies have been written evaluating Hamlet, and his profoundly searching soliloquies have been exhaustively analyzed. Most authorities agree that Hamlet is an exceedingly complex individual who, though gifted with the sword, is given more to philosophizing than to direct action. Hamlet does not view the world, himself, or even the villain of this play in a simple detached manner; he studies and restudies the behavior of his fellow men, as well as his own behavior. His many soliloquies on his procrastination in executing the command of his father's ghost ("To be or not to be" is the most renowned) testify to his failure to come to terms with his inner being. While he accumulates more and more evidence of Claudius' obvious guilt, he constantly returns to the theme of his mother's remarriage—a source of pain equally as unbearable as the circumstances of his father's death. It is ironic that the one time Hamlet acts decisively without some meditation, he kills Polonius, mistakenly thinking him to be the king. When Hamlet does at last kill Claudius, he himself is dying, and he is spontaneously provoked by Gertrude's death and Laertes' accusation.

Hamlet is a man of integrity, obviously honored and beloved by his people, but he sacrifices even Ophelia to his overwhelming preoccupation with Claudius and Gertrude. The more Hamlet becomes obsessed with the deed he knows he must do, the less he is able to execute it. Hamlet is a truly heroic figure, but his need to dwell on his tragic situation, led to his own death.

Claudius

Claudius, the king, has murdered his brother, Hamlet's father, and married Queen Gertrude. Claudius is contrasted with Hamlet as a man of action. If evil is essential to the realization of a goal, then Claudius will sacrifice the ethic for the end. He does not commit evil carelessly, but is quite ready to waive morality in the light of necessity. He is strong-minded, passionate, and above all, directional. He makes his plans and proceeds accordingly. He is intelligent in his understanding of human motivation, and knows how to manipulate those around him. He is fully aware of Hamlet's suspicions and the motive behind Hamlet's supposed madness. Only twice, once in an aside to Polonius' description of Ophelia, and more forcibly in the scene where he is praying, does Claudius verbalize any qualms of conscience, and even here, the thoughts are not allowed to interfere with the resolution. Claudius is astute and calculating, ambitious and ruthless in his pursuit of power. These traits, in combination with Hamlet's apparent uncertainty, delay his death until Laertes' accusation in the final scene of the play.

Gertrude

Gertrude, queen of Denmark, wife of Claudius and mother of Hamlet, is innocent of the murder of her husband, Hamlet's father. She obviously loved and was loved and revered by her first husband. But the combination of her own meekness and the strength of Claudius' passion and power to act have led her to this second marriage. She had questioned neither her husband's untimely death nor her hasty remarriage, accepting both as natural to the order of things, until Hamlet's return to Denmark. Now she is "cleft . . . in twain," torn between her love for her son Hamlet and her allegiance to her husband and King, Claudius. Hamlet plants in her a guilt she did not feel; she is tormented by both her divided loyalties of the present, and her sudden conscious recognition of the immorality of her remarriage. Unable to do more than show anguish at a pain new to the hitherto evenness of her life, Gertrude allows Claudius to plan their joint treatment of Hamlet: their attitudes toward his madness, the trip to England, the duel with Laertes. In all these events she is outside the planned treachery, yet she unwittingly conforms to Claudius' schemings, and in the end, dies a victim of the poisoned drink intended for Hamlet.

Ophelia

Ophelia, daughter of Polonius and Laertes' sister, embodies the romantic notion of womanhood: she is beautiful, sweet, industrious, gentle. She loves Hamlet, and initially, believes in his love for her. But when her brother and father lecture her on the impossibility of this love and her foolishness, she bows to their authority and withdraws.

Hamlet's "madness" first confuses her; then it wounds and terrifies her. Although she reveals an intelligence in her conversations with Laertes and Polonius, and in her behavior at "the play," she is completely unable to comprehend the treachery of the court and the complex behavior of Hamlet. Direct, honest, and trusting, the deceitful intrigues which surround her, combined with the sudden death of her beloved father, throw her into a state of madness. Ophelia's drowning, described by the queen as an accident resulting from her distraught behavior, is sometimes thought to have been the suicide of an innocent, unworldly maiden who can no longer cope with the complexity of her life. There is little factual proof for this latter interpretation of her death though.

Polonius

Polonius, father of Laertes and Ophelia, is the lord chamberlain in the court of Claudius. Although not an evil man, Polonius is nevertheless cynical and self-seeking in his eagerness to receive the favor of the king and queen. Pragmatic and realistic, he gives his departing son advice calculated to make Laertes a friend of everyone and offensive to none. In like manner, he instructs Ophelia to ignore the attentions of a man placed as highly as Hamlet. He is convinced that the prince, above Ophelia socially, is only selfishly motivated. Polonius' craving to be esteemed by the king and queen, coupled with his limited sensitivity, leads him to verbosity and clumsy meddling. In an attempt to ingratiate himself, he offers to spy upon the interview between the queen and Hamlet. Startled by what he takes to be the queen's cry for help, he reveals his presence to Hamlet, who, believing the king to be thus hidden, draws his sword and kills Polonius through the curtains.

Laertes

Laertes, Polonius' son and brother of Ophelia, is somewhat cynical like his father in advising Ophelia of the impossibility of love with Prince Hamlet. But Laertes has a basic courage and honesty. If he is rash and hot-headed, it is because he takes it upon himself to avenge first his father's death, and then his sister's insanity. He seems to have had a youthful fling in Paris, but he returns to Denmark to the serious responsibility of manhood—that is, to uncover his father's murderer and to avenge Polonius' almost-secret, unhonored burial. While his wrath leads him to use an unprotected and poisoned foil in his duel with Hamlet, he is more Claudius' dupe than his co-conspirator. His conscience troubles him during the exchange, and when he falls victim as a result of a confusion of weapons, he confesses his treachery to Hamlet, and dies indicting the king.

Horatio

Horatio, a young Dane and friend of Hamlet, has been away at the University of Wittenberg and has returned for the funeral of Hamlet's father. His is a most sympathetic portrait: a man who is both a scholar and a person of irrefutable good character. Although there is always recognition of Hamlet's princely status, Horatio is treated as a true friend by the prince and becomes his confidant. He is drawn as a learned man, of even disposition, truly just and honorable without being falsely moved by passion. It is Horatio who first informs Hamlet of the appearance of his father's ghost. The prince later confides to Horatio the bloody deeds of his uncle, his grief over the queen's marriage, the treachery of Rosencrantz and Guildenstern, and his plan to observe Claudius at "the play." Concerned for the safety of his friend, Horatio tries to dissuade Hamlet from dueling with Laertes, and in his selfless loyalty, wants to drink the poison as Hamlet is dying. The prince restrains him, and Horatio remains to tell Fortinbras and all the world of the tragedies which have occurred.

Rosencrantz and Guildenstern

Two contemporaries of Hamlet, and companions of his youth, they are recalled to Denmark by Claudius and act as his willing tools. Their feigned friendship with Hamlet, which the prince knows to be false, is typical of their servile behavior in deference to social rank. Hamlet likens them to a "sponge," which absorbs the orders and rewards of the King and eventually, is squeezed dry into nothingness. Hamlet uncovers their deceitfulness and ironically arranges for their deaths in place of his—a just reward for their disloyalty.

Fortinbras

Fortinbras, prince of Norway, has embarked upon a military venture, designed to regain for his country the lands forfeited by his father in combat with Hamlet's father. He is dissuaded from this enterprise by Claudius' warning to his old uncle in Norway, who restrains Fortinbras and sets him upon a different course of attack. At the close of the play, Fortinbras reveals admiration for Hamlet's princely qualities, and sorrow for the tragic deaths about him. Nonetheless, he makes it quite clear that he will assert his right of ascendancy to the now-empty throne.

Osric

He is a young courtier who carries Claudius' message to Hamlet, proposing the duel between Hamlet and Laertes. Osric has the outwardly verbose and superficial manner of the courtier. Hamlet mocks him in their interchange, but Osric is insensitive to the intended ridicule.

Questions and Answers on the Characters

Question 1.
From the play, quoting where you can, show Hamlet to be excitable, affectionate, melancholic, sarcastic and refined.

Answer
EXCITABLE: When the ghost appears to him, his fate cries out:

And makes each pretty artery in this body
As hardy as the Nemean lion's nerve.

The ghost finds him "apt," and indeed, at that moment, when "desperate with imagination," he longed to sweep to his revenge "With wings as swift/As meditation or the thoughts of love."

He was still under the influence of excitement produced by his interview with the ghost when he decided to assume the role of a madman.

After the trial of the play, in "the very witching time of night," he could:

drink hot blood,
And do such bitter business as the day
Would quake to look on.

In such a mood, he cruelly abused his mother and murdered Polonius, mistaking him for the king. At other times his excitable nature was roused to passion by the player's speech, by the example of Fortinbras, and by the sight of Laertes' boisterous grief at Ophelia's grave. On this last occasion he falls into uncontrollable rage:

Woo't weep? woo't fight? woo't fast? woo't tear thyself?
Woo't drink up essil? eat a crocodile
I'll do't,

he exclaims, and his actions show that the violence of his emotion has in it something dangerous that wisdom may well fear. But his passion was as short-lived as it was violent. To Horatio he repented, and promised to make amends to Laertes when the opportunity should arise. All his sudden actions (the dooming to death of his schoolfellows, the murder of the king, the snatching of the bowl of poison from Horatio), were performed on impulse and in sudden inspirations of excited feeling.

AFFECTIONATE: He respected, admired, and loved his father, whom he describes as his "dear murthered father," and of whom he says:

'A was a man, take him for all in all,
I shall not look upon his like again.

Hamlet had loved Ophelia tenderly and she responded with gentle, clinging affection. At her graveside, in passionate words, he exclaims:

Forty thousand brothers
Could not with all their quantity of love
Make up my sum.

But his affection for Horatio was more deep-seated. In his chosen friend's nature he found something that made up for his own over-sensitivity. In him he found relief from his sense of loneliness. He shows his affection for Horatio by saying of him:

Since my dear soul was mistress of my choice,
And could of men distinguish, her election
Hath sealed thee for herself.

Hamlet's gentle nature feels an affectionate sympathy even for Laertes in his grief; he "freely embraces his offered love like love, and by the image of his own cause sees the portraiture of his."

MELANCHOLIC: He first appears in the drama dressed in solemn mourning, with "dejected 'haviour of the visage," the clouds still hanging on him. The queen urges him:

Do not for ever with thy veiled lids
Seek for thy noble father in the dust.

In his first soliloquy he utters the despondent words:

O that this too, too sullied flesh would melt,
Thaw, and resolve itself into a dew!

He regards the world as a prison, the earth "an unweeded garden," "a sterile promontory," the heavens as "a foul and pestilent congregation of vapours". He loses all his humor and "walks for

68

hours together" in the palace hall, his general behavior the picture of melancholy. "Look where sadly the poor wretch comes reading," said the queen on one occasion. After the player's recitation he refers to his own melancholy mood, and considers the possibility that he may have been all along the dupe of the devil, who:

> Out of my weakness and my melancholy,
> As he is very potent with such spirits,
> Abuses me to damn me.

He seems to revel in thoughts of death and suicide, and from his interview with Ophelia, the king concludes that:

> There's something in his soul
> O'er which his melancholy sits on brood.

All his fits of impulsive action are followed by periods of melancholy and despair. After his first interview with the ghost, he cursed his fate; after the death of Polonius, he wept; after his passionate scene with Laertes, his silence did "sit, drooping." In the last act, his conversation with Laertes, and the solemn reflections which fall from his lips in the graveyard scene, show the melancholy cast of thought that had now become habitual with him.

SARCASTIC: Many sarcastic images, comparisons, and allusions escape from Hamlet in his varying moods. At times his sarcasm is witty and humorous, as when he fools Polonius (Act II, Sc. 2; Act III, Sc. 2), or ridicules the courtiers (Act II, Sc. 2; Act IV, Sc. 2); when he indulges in trifling conversation with Ophelia (Act III, Sc. 2). At other times he expresses himself with bitter sarcasm, showing his undisguised contempt for the hypocrisy, deceit, and shallowness with which he is surrounded. He speaks of the king in terms of scornful disgust: he is "a vice of kings," "a villain and a cutpurse," "a king of shreds and patches," a "thing of nothing," who delights in revels and in drunkenness.

During the interlude, and in the presence of the king, Hamlet seems to find some compensation for his inaction in sarcastic utterances:

> 'Tis a knavish piece of work; but what o' that? Your Majesty,
> and we that have free souls, it touches us not; let the galled
> jade wince, our withers are unwrung.

Even the queen, his mother, is not spared, although once he dearly loved her; now, he treats her with contempt. With cruel irony he addresses her:

For who that's but a queen, fair, sober, wise,
Would from a paddock, from a bat, a gib,
Such dear concernings hide?

On the point of leaving for England, he sarcastically takes leave of his father with the words, "Farewell, dear mother;" and in the grave-yard scene, his aversion to all that is false or affected is shown by his sarcastic and ironical allusions to politicians, courtiers, and lawyers. Pointing to the skull he holds in his hand, he says:

Now get you to my lady's chamber, and tell her, let her paint an inch thick, to this favour must she come; make her laugh at that.

REFINED: He has no sympathy with the revels and drunkenness of his age (Act I, Sc. 4). A man endowed with "noble and most sovereign reason," he associated with scholars and artists. He composed verses, and carried books about with him. He possessed "The courtier's, soldier's, scholar's eye, tongue, sword," and was:

The expectancy and rose of the fair state,
The glass of fashion and the mould of form,
The observed of all observers.

By nature, he preferred meditation and philosophy, and the emotional side of his character was no less highly developed than the intellectual. To the gravedigger he was mad, but to Horatio he was "a noble heart." He was deeply hurt by his mother's lack of shame and modesty, and the king's grossness and lust were more revolting to him than the crime of murder.

Question 2.
How is Polonius viewed by the other major characters in the play?

Answer
Polonius is the adviser of the king, whom he serves to the best of his ability with fidelity and zeal. He possesses a certain amount of the confidence of his royal master, who, however, consults him more often on domestic than on state affairs. As a result of his long experience, he has acquired a considerable share of worldly wisdom, which he is fond of exhibiting on all occasions, whether called for or not. The king thinks of him "as of a man faithful and honorable"; the queen speaks of him as a "good old man." Laertes's love for him is such that, to avenge his death, he "hazards both the worlds," and Ophelia, in her madness, retains none but the sweetest memories of him.

Such is the light in which he was regarded by those whom natural affection blinded to his defects, or by people who saw in him a means of serving their own ends. Hamlet, however, brought an unbiased judgment to bear upon his character, and that he was not very much mistaken in his unfavorable opinion of the "wretched, rash, intruding fool," will be evident from the following considerations:

(1) Polonius was deceitful and cunning, as is shown by the indirect, crooked methods he adopted for obtaining any information he needed: he hired spies to watch Laertes when he was in Paris; he used his daughter as an instrument for discovering the cause of Hamlet's madness; and he was unscrupulous enough to play the part of a spy himself.

(2) He is suspicious and prying, meddles with everything, listens to slander about his daughter, mistrusts his son, and boasts to the king of his ability to find "where truth is hid, though it were hid, indeed, within the centre."

(3) He is superficial, shallow, conceited, and long-winded, he prides himself on his knowledge and judgment, his literary, critical, and histrionic ability. Yet all the while he is exposing his own folly and ignorance.

(4) He is ignorant of true wisdom, and entirely misunderstands Hamlet's nature and actions. He sins against the canons of good taste even while propounding them. He is, in fact, one of those "seeming wise men," of whom it has been said that they "may make shift to get opinion, but let no man choose them for employment."

Question 3.

Describe the character of Gertrude in terms of her innocence.

Answer

Despite some uncertainty at times, the verdict of Gertrude's complicity in the murder of her first husband and in continued intrigue is "not guilty." Not only has the ghost (proved trustworthy) counseled Hamlet to "leave her to heaven," but we realize her lack of knowledge of Claudius' actions and intentions during the scene with Hamlet in her bedchamber and during the dueling scene. She has been maneuvered by her second husband into moves which aid his cause. The picture of the queen that arises is that of a gullible, somewhat slow-witted, easily manipulated, changeable, and inconstant woman. She has been wooed and won over easily by her husband's brother, perhaps even before his murder (probably through flattery). She avoids self-accusation and analysis, and seems incapable of coming to grips with unpleasantness. She grasps at easy answers and makes excuses for everyone. Therefore, the effect on her of the interview with Hamlet, (Act III, Sc. 4) and of Ophelia's madness and suicide is confusion and bewilderment. In a sense, she ironically balances Ophelia in their mixture of immorality and innocence; or, to look at it differently, the queen is as unsuspicious at the wrong time as Polonius is suspicious of the wrong circumstances. There is little to admire in Gertrude, regardless of what pardons we make for her.

Question 4.

Briefly describe Rosencrantz and Guildenstern, Osric, and the gravediggers.

Answer

Rosencrantz and Guildenstern are important as representing a type rather than for any actions or utterances of their own. They represent the type of fawning, flattering courtiers that "soak up the king's countenance, his rewards, his authorities," and are ready for any mean and immoral work in his service. Such characters may be supposed to have had a good education—they were Hamlet's school-fellows—and to have been well versed in the arts and accomplishments of a conventional society. They are an indivisible couple, each deriving support and confidence from the presence of the other. Devoid of all originality, they form their opinions on all subjects in accordance with the fashion of the day, being well satisfied if they can only get "the tune of the time and outward habit of encounter." Their knowledge is superficial and their intelligence mediocre, so that they are easily foiled by Hamlet in any argument or combat of wit. They are not of the stuff that great criminals are made, having neither power of initiation, nor courage, nor acuteness of judgment, nor shrewdness. They are fools rather than knaves, and though they meet with a more severe punishment than they deserve, we are conscious of no pity for them.

Osric is a fashionable gentleman of the court. He has much land, and therefore stands high in the king's favor. He is a friend of Laertes, whose qualities he admires, and for whom he acts as second in the duel. His language is affected and pedantic. He deals in high-flown compliments, and makes a great parade of politeness. When his shallowness and superficiality are exposed by Hamlet, he either does not, or will not, perceive that he is the object of Hamlet's satire. There is some doubt as to whether or not he was aware of the treachery against Hamlet's life, but we cannot fail to regard with some suspicion the man who gave the combatants their foils, and to whom Laertes, when wounded with the poisoned point, exclaims:

Why, as a woodcock to mine own springe, Osric,
I am justly killed with mine own treachery.
                                        (Act V, Sc. 2, 295-96)

The gravediggers are introduced as they are discussing the legality of Ophelia's burial in sanctified ground. On this, as on other topics, they express their opinions with almost socialistic freedom. This tendency toward socialism is perceived by Hamlet, who says, ''the age is grown so picked that the toe of the peasant comes so near the heel of the courtier, he galls his kibe.'' These ale-washed wits have lost all feeling of their business, and sing and crack jokes over their dismal work, as though gravedigging were the most pleasant trade on earth. Like other characters in the play, the first clown seeks to show his cleverness and ingenuity in words; he has caught the trick of the age, and can reason and philosophize with the prince of philosophers.

Structure

Methods of Analyzing Structure

For art to exist in any real way, something has to be *made*. A given work of art, therefore, has some sort of definite structure, even if that structure is an abstract kind of formless entity. The structure of literary works of art is not something uniform. From genre to genre, and within each genre, there are virtually countless kinds of structures. It would be idle work to attempt to discuss the structures of *King Lear* and *The Catcher in the Rye* in the same way. The purpose of this section is to familiarize students with some of the ways in which we can discuss structure, with a particular interest in a Shakespearean drama. After introducing several methods of analyzing structure, we will illustrate the ways in which these methods can be used in answering particular questions.

1. Analysis

The first place to start an analysis of structure is in consideration of plot. If plot is, as Aristotle stated, the first principle and soul of tragedy, it seems obvious that we should come to certain conclusions about the plot before passing on to other more sophisticated dimensions. In a certain sense, structure is another word for plot. Both describe what *is*; that is, both direct us to *what happens when,* which is the heart of the drama. The structure, in other words, is the way in which the events of the play are put together. The turning points, reversals, or alterations within the action of the play are all presented in a definite way for a definite purpose. The student's task is to begin by establishing clearly in his mind the *order* of the events and then go on to *explanations* of that order. Most dramatists are, fortunately, logical as well as entertaining. We are not so much called upon to discover their intentions, as rather, the logical reasons for things happening when they do. In short, then, the first way in which to begin an analysis of structure is to delineate and explain the plot in all of its changes and reversals.

2. Synthesis

Whereas in ''Analysis'' we were concerned with presenting the physical division of the work into its parts, as discovered in the plot, now we should make an effort to explain the development of the connections between the parts. What are the elements which link the various stages of the play? If we are considering a tragedy, how does the dramatist allow the play to flow from preparations for the "fall," through the "fall," and finally into the aftermath? Where are the *key* turning points in the plot? How has the dramatist prepared us in the beginning for what will arrive in the ending? In other words, in synthesis, we attempt to draw all of the parts of the play together. It is one thing to divide the work into its parts, and another to explain the ways in which those parts have been logically connected.

More often than not, the student will find that the *motives of the characters* provide the links between the parts. X happens when it does, because Character Y has certain motives. Particularly in tragedy, we discover the importance of characters' motives in explaining the logic of the plot. Obviously some of the parts of the plot will be joined through contrived "accidents," such as a chance meeting or the discovery of a stolen letter. Since plays are primarily about people, however, more often than not the people in the play become the organizing factors. One character's greed or another one's jealousy will often be sufficient explanation for the fact that everything in the play happens when it does. But whether the student concentrates on character motivation or on the chance events of fortune, he must always be asking whether the structure seems molded in not only a logical but an esthetic way. And this leads us to our next consideration.

3. Esthetic Unity

When the student has divided the work into structural sections, and explained the way in which these sections are held together, he must then decide whether or not the entire framework has esthetic unity. Is the ending artistically derived from the opening? Do the motives of the characters adequately explain their actions? Is there any sort of inconsistency between the characters' motives and actions which the dramatist leaves unexplained? In "Analysis" we divide the action of the play into its logical sections, but now we try to evaluate and to criticize. A good tragedy should have an *introduction, rising action,* a *climax, falling action,* and a *catastrophe.* That is, we need to be introduced to some of the characters, be told about things which have happened recently before the play's opening, and in general given enough information to understand what happens *in* the play.

In the *rising action* are certain events or revealed attitudes which lead logically into the *climax* or chief turning point in the play. There is usually some sort of *exciting action,* something, some reason which sets the rising action in motion. Sometimes it is the challenge to solve a riddle, other times the desire to avenge a slain relative. But there is always some reason which causes the action to commence. After the climax, certain events lead—and usually quite swiftly—to the final catastrophe, which is usually a multiple death or at least the death of the central character. The structure of most classical and Shakespearean tragedy is in accord with this formula and thus keeping these terms in mind often makes it easier to discuss the structure of *any* play, even if there are modifications which must be made.

Whether or not a tragedy moves skilfully through these stages or their explicit equivalent is the factor upon which our evaluation of the esthetic unity will usually depend. For example, it would not be esthetically satisfying if the death of the hero simply arrived without any particular climax preceding it. We need to feel the building of certain emotions which are responsible for the catastrophe, and without such a building we feel cheated.

4. Relations of Parts to Whole

In all of these approaches, and in countless others which the student will be able to devise for himself, we are concerned in one way or another with the relationship between the parts and the whole. We want to arrive at an understanding of structure by dividing a work, putting it back together, shaking it, and finally coming up with explanations of how it "works." We want to be able to say this play has the following structure and this is why it is or is not successful. Any given scene or act should contribute significantly to the overall structure of a play, for a play is too short for much waste of time. In other words, we address ourselves to the relationship between each of the parts and the whole in order to arrive at an understanding of the whole.

Some critics follow the general approach to the construction of Shakespeare's tragedies outlined and developed by A. C. Bradley in his famous lectures. Bradley explains how a Shakespearean tragedy always depicts some sort of *conflict* between competing forces which ends in *catastrophe.* Every play has three large parts. The first is the *exposition* or early part of the play where the dramatist presents us with certain information, introduces us to the world of the drama and to the characters. The second section is devoted to the complication or *conflict*—its beginnings, changes, reversals of advantage between the competing forces—and the third shows us the results of the conflict, that is, the catastrophe or conclusion. Often, Shakespeare gets the attention of his audience in the opening of a play with a dramatic event—such as the appearance of the ghost of Hamlet's father—and then slows the pace to provide us with certain necessary facts, usually presented through low-keyed conversations with little background action. In short, though, Shakespeare maintains the conflict throughout the play in various ways. There is constant alternation between our fears and our hopes as first one side is up, then another opposing one gathers momentum. The large three-fold way of viewing the construction of a Shakespearean play is often very useful, although not all of his plays fit the three-part division easily.

Questions and Answers on Structure

Question 5.

Outline the purpose and major events of each act, as they relate to the structure of *Hamlet*.

Answer

As in all of Shakespeare's plays, *Hamlet* is divided into five acts.

ACT I: INTRODUCTION: The setting (time and place) of the action is presented, and we are introduced to the central themes and characters of the play.

ACT II: DEVELOPMENT: Hamlet's plan to pretend that he is mad is put into action; Claudius schemes with Polonius to uncover the reasons behind Hamlet's strange behavior.

ACT III: CLIMAX: The Mouse-trap is "sprung" and Claudius is proven guilty (at least to Hamlet's satisfaction); Polonius is killed; the queen breaks down under Hamlet's merciless indictment.

ACT IV: DENOUNCEMENT: The results of the crisis and the procession of events toward the final catastrophe are presented. Hamlet is sent to England; Ophelia becomes insane and then dies; Laertes returns and becomes a party to Claudius' plot to kill Hamlet.

ACT V: CONCLUSION: The play moves swiftly towards a final catastrophe involving the deaths of all the chief characters, except Horatio and Fortinbras.

Question 6.

In what way can Fortinbras be considered a character whose chief function in the play is to serve its structural demands?

Answer

It is significant that the play is framed between the military preparations of Fortinbras, mentioned in the first scene, and the timely arrival of Fortinbras in the final scene, when he claims the throne of Denmark and has Hamlet nobly carried from the stage with "soldiers' music and rites of war."

Hamlet and Fortinbras never actually meet during the play. Fortinbras is just spoken of in Act I, Sc. 1; he leaves before Hamlet enters in Act IV, Sc. 4; and he arrives at the Danish court just after Hamlet's death in the last scene. Yet Hamlet does come across Fortinbras' army in Act IV, Sc. 4, and this incident serves to contrast—both for the audience and for Hamlet himself—the daring, honorable and assertive character of Fortinbras with the uncertain and aggressive Hamlet. Witnessing Fortinbras' troops preparing to fight for a cause which, to Hamlet, seems of so little concern, inspires the Danish prince to renew his efforts to seek revenge on Claudius for a cause which is of comparably greater importance. In Fortinbras' efforts to regain his father's lost territory and Hamlet's struggle to avenge the wrongs committed against his father by Claudius, there is an evident parallel. Each son accomplishes his mission by the end of the play, and though Hamlet forfeits his life for this purpose, he dies an honorable death, as Fortinbras confirms when he accords Hamlet soldiers' rites. It is by Fortinbras that we can measure the change in Hamlet from the adolescent scholar at the beginning of the play, to the young man more mature in thought and prepared for action in Act IV, Sc. 4, to the brave and heroic avenger figure he becomes just before his death.

Question 7.

The structure of drama is sometimes thought to be based on the principle of action followed by reaction. Cite examples in *Hamlet* of a character's own actions backfiring or reacting against him—a pattern that the Greeks called nemesis.

Answer

Hamlet's unsuspicious generosity is certainly mistaken in the last scene. He ought to have known his uncle by that time.

Gertrude's faithlessness to her husband's memory and her hasty marriage with this man she loves so madly, eventually brings about her death through his treachery to her son.

Claudius' original crime necessitates further crimes and he dies as a result of his own treachery by the hand of his nephew, the son of the man he murdered.

Polonius' passion for spying brings about his own death, quite unregretted by the audience, who are inclined to think, "served you right!"

Ophelia's too ready obedience to her petty-minded father starts the train of circumstances that lead to her insanity and death.

Laertes brings on his own death through his treacherous action in illegally removing the button from his foil and poisoning the point.

Notice that in each of the above instances, it is a character's own weakness that causes his undoing. This notion of a flaw in a person's character bringing disaster to that person is an important element in the working of nemesis.

Question 8.

What is the purpose of the graveyard scene in terms of the play's structure?

Answer

The graveyard scene is spectacular and gripping in itself, and though it does not advance the actual action of the play to any great extent, it provides a gleam of humor in this grim atmosphere. Further, it provides another lull before the last great storm. This scene also shows that Hamlet really was intensely in love with Ophelia and that he had purposely suppressed the romance while it interfered with his mission. He was a sufferer, too, though the effects of this whole situation were disastrous for her.

Question 9.

Classical tragedy observed what Aristotle called the *unity of time* (that is, the action of the tragedy was supposed to take place within one day). What length of time is covered in *Hamlet?*

Answer

The time of the play is seven days represented on the stage—or eight if the reader prefers to assign a separate day to the last scene—with two intervals.

Day 1: Act I, Scene 1 to Scene 3.
Day 2: Act I, Scene 4 and Scene 5.
> An interval of over two months.

Day 3: Act II, Scene 1 and Scene 2.
Day 4: Act III, Scene 1 to Scene 4; Act IV, Scene 1 to Scene 3.
Day 5: Act IV, Scene 4.
> An interval of perhaps a week.

Day 6: Act IV, Scene 5 to Scene 7.
Day 7: Act V, Scene 1 and Scene 2.

Meaning

Methods of Analyzing Meaning

Sometimes, it is noted, we forget about the forest because we are too busy looking at the individual trees. In this sense we are apt to avoid commenting on the fundamental meaning of a work of art because we are so concerned with character, structure, and style. Although it is obvious that we cannot avoid completely the implications of the various components of a play as they bear on its meaning, the fact remains that we should take the time to make some sort of general statement about what Shakespeare is trying to tell us. And once we have decided on the meaning, we then can attempt to evaluate the play, to measure it against other plays which treat the same ideas.

1. Explaining the Theme

The student's first task is to denote and explain the central theme of the play. This is not always easily done and, in fact, one sometimes must conclude that there are several themes combined throughout the play. Sometimes—but not often—there is no theme at all. The theme is the central and major idea of the work; in drama the theme is usually an abstract idea or argument which becomes real and concrete through the actions of the characters; as critics we must translate action back into thought, just as the playwright first translated thought into action.

2. Conventions

Usually the dramatist transports us into the world of the play through various dramatic conventions. We must ask how we, the audience, are transported into the minds of the characters. We must try to determine how we are made to believe certain ideas—how, in other words, does the dramatist convince us of the meaning of something? If we are led to believe that love is evil, how does the dramatist lead us to this belief? Meaning is not something easily determined and its presentation must often be clearly understood in order for us to determine precisely *why* such-and-such appears to be true.

3. Unusual or Conventional

The student must answer a basic question when discussing meaning: is it a conventional idea or an unusual one? For example, if the theme of the play is that revenge often only leads to further misery, we can speak of the theme as being "conventional." That is, the idea of the play is one which has been presented many times; it is an *established theme*. On the other hand, a play's main point might be very unusual. If a play's argument is that people who live in glass houses *should* throw stones, the play is making an unusual or uncommon point. Almost every play can be described, in its meaning, as being either conventional or unconventional; and once this is done, the student must explain the ways in which it is or is not conventional.

4. Relating Plot to Meaning

Probably the best way to begin one's analysis of the meaning of a play is to trace very briefly the main plot development in the play. In other words, we need to make a short synopsis of the action before we can make a general statement about the meaning. Then, as we become more particular in our comments on the meaning, we should introduce more particular use of the plot; in other words, we are concerned with making the *level* of our analysis correspond to the level of our explication of the plot. The broad statement needs a broad grasp of the plot, while the "fine points" need more particular textual backing.

5. Logic

As a final check on our understanding of the play we should make some attempt to ascertain whether or not the meaning is logically developed. If the theme somehow seems contradicted by the behavior of one or more characters, or if the relationship between two of the characters argues against the main idea of the play, then we have a problem of logic—which can mean either that the dramatist has not done an expert job, or that we have misunderstood the meaning of the play. If our "interpretation" of a play is correct, we should be able to demonstrate logically why it is correct, while, on the other hand, if our interpretation is incorrect, a final check of the logic will force us into reconsideration and probably a revised, improved understanding of the play.

Questions and Answers on Meaning

Question 10.
Relate Hamlet's mental development to the meaning of the play.

Answer
To trace the steps by which Hamlet arrives at a resolution to his uncertain state of mind is, according to Hardin Craig, to master the meaning of the play. Hamlet progresses towards both action and the achievement of peace of mind, with Horatio standing on one side of him as a man who has self-possession, and Fortinbras on the other as a man to whom action is instinctive. It is through Hamlet's struggle to act, and to act wisely, that the larger concept of man's complex nature is illustrated.

The soliloquies in the play mark the stages of Hamlet's mental development. The first soliloquy in Act I, Scene 2, 129-59 shows Hamlet to be outraged at the treachery of Claudius and the "incestuous" marriage of his mother, but he is unable to act upon his convictions. After meeting with the Ghost, who prompts Hamlet to seek revenge, he is determined to act; however, Hamlet's feelings at this point (Act I, Scene 5, 97-112) are not guided by reason. Action alone will not satisfy the demands on Hamlet, since it is wise and appropriate action that he must undertake. In the famous "To be or not to be" soliloquy, Hamlet's excitement is calmed, and he achieves a balance between action and inaction when he wonders:

> Whether 'tis nobler in the mind to suffer
> The slings and arrows of outrageous fortune,
> Or to take arms against a sea of troubles,
> And by opposing end them?

Hamlet then progresses to the point of being overcalculating in Act III, Scene 3, 73-96, when he deliberately delays murdering Claudius at prayer because to kill the king now would "this same villain send /To heaven." Despite Hamlet's expressed concern with commiting the act properly, he acts rashly when he kills Polonius in Act III, Scene 4, and after this mistaken deed, a period of inaction on Hamlet's part follows. But after witnessing the marching of troops commanded by Fortinbras, Hamlet, in another soliloquy (Act IV, Scene 4, 32-66), once again recognizes the need to "spur [his] dull revenge." In Act V,

Hamlet's conversation with Horatio in the churchyard regarding the value of life shows that he has attained a more philosophical state of mind. Later in this act, his bitter outburst at the grave of Ophelia reveals the full development of his passionate nature as well. By the end of the play, Hamlet demonstrates both the self-knowledge and spirit of action necessary to carry out his revenge on Claudius in a fitting manner.

Question 11.

How does the question of appearance and reality affect the meaning of the play?

Answer

A major question for man is: What is truth? It involves such further questions as what is reality? How does one separate what appears to be truthful or real or absolute from what actually is? How can one determine what actually is truthful or real or absolute? During the Elizabethan Age the question was most compelling because of the advances of science. The certainties of the past were being disproved or at least modified. New celestial bodies were being discovered; new means of combating illnesses were being found; new concepts of the earth and its inhabitants came with the expansion of navigational exploration; and new views of God's creation necessarily followed. With universes beyond the no longer geocentric universe of medieval tradition, where could man place himself in the scheme of creation? The Englishman was only one man of many on earth; the earth was only one planet of many in the universe; the universe was only one in how many universes. That which was truth had been shown not to be truth.

In *Hamlet* the problems of truth and the nature of man appear on every page: Is the ghost good or evil? Is his story true or false? Is Hamlet's madness real or feigned? Is Polonius' advice wisdom or folly? Is his interpretation of Hamlet's relationship with Ophelia correct? Is she innocent or loose of character? The way in which appearance is taken for reality is underscored by the acting of Polonius, Rosencrantz, Guildenstern, and Hamlet, and by the play-within-a-play and the discussion of plays and actors. Should "this goodly frame, the earth," be thought a "most excellent canopy . . . fretted with golden fire" or "a sterile promontory . . . a foul and pestilent congregation of vapours" (Act II, Sc. 2, 306 ff.)? Hamlet follows these questions with musings on man: "what is this quintessence of dust?" He concludes (Act IV, Sc. 4) that a man is one who uses his capability and godlike reason; that person is a beast who simply sleeps and feeds. Hamlet has come to realize that man is noble in reason and the paragon of animals when he finds "quarrel in a straw/When honor's at the stake." Truth seems to reside in the existential idea: all that individual man knows is that he exists. For man truth can be only that which magnifies him in moral spheres. The essence of truth is thus divorced from substance and from the means through which substance appears.

Question 12.

Consider the theme of honor as it relates to the characters and actions of Hamlet, Laertes, and Fortinbras.

Answer

The parallel situations of Hamlet, Laertes, and Fortinbras examine the theme of honor and honorable action. Each seeks a restitution of loss from the death of a father, but the course that each takes is to be evaluated by the audience. Laertes seeks revenge known as *lex talionis,* "an eye for an eye;" but what casts this retributive justice into disrepute is the deceptive and murderous means by which he hopes to achieve justice: poison-tipped foils. This action can be classified only as evil: to seek to avenge a wrong by vicious action is abhorrent. Laertes does not "duplicate" Hamlet's ill action against Polonius (nor should he), thereby nullifying it, if successful. His honorable course would be challenge but without deceit. Fortinbras' course is an honorable one: he acts to regain the position of fame and material being that his father had. He accepts a challenge in the same sphere of action which his father had made and lost. His course is reasoned and public, but it does involve "the imminent death of twenty thousand men . . . for a fantasy and trick of fame" (Act IV, Sc. 4, 60-61).

Hamlet's course alters from indecision to action pulled in two directions. First, it is tempered by demands of proof; second, it is influenced by reason and then by emotion; third, it is necessary to reverse deception, and to make and accept challenge, first emotionally and then rationally. The need for proof places Hamlet in a different situation from those of Laertes and Fortinbras. His emotional course echoes Laertes', and his reversal of the king's deceptive act has similarities to Laertes' villainy. The results of the first are unjustified, and thus we see emotional response as wrong; but the results of the second are justified, and thus we see reasoned response as acceptable. Note that after acceptance of the king's guilt, Hamlet moves from reason (the prayer scene) to emotion (the killing of Polonius) to reasoned resolution, followed by acts of reason (the dispatch of Rosencrantz and Guildenstern), emotion (the argument at Ophelia's grave), and reason (the duel).

The theme of honor makes clear that action to correct a wrong should be reasoned, not emotional; it should be a reversal of the wrong as exactly as is honorably possible; and it should partake of public action and particularly that considered noble and commanding of respect. God's justice is accomplished by the various deaths and the ascendancy of Fortinbras to the throne. Hamlet can not live and have justice prevail, for he has erred in killing Polonius. Yet his death is ennobled by his final honorable actions in correcting the sources of rottenness within the state.

Question 13.

How is the theme of love presented in *Hamlet?*

Answer

For the most part faith is missing from *Hamlet.* The king, the queen, Rosencrantz, Guildenstern, Polonius, and Laertes are not trustworthy; the ghost's truthfulness must be established; and Ophelia proves unfaithful to Hamlet. Only Horatio is to be trusted and remains faithful. Without faith love cannot exist. Polonius talks a great deal about Ophelia and Hamlet's love, but all, including Ophelia, do not recognize his statements of faith and love in his letter read to the court by Polonius.

On the other hand there is Ophelia's obedience to her father and her remorse at his death; and there is the compassion of the player for Hecuba. In the final act we hear Hamlet coming to an answer for his question, "what is this quintessence of dust," as he observes the gravedigger and the noble dust of one who might have been an Alexander. The concept of love which is missing in Hamlet's makeup and which is developed in the play is charity, or brotherly love. Hamlet seeks Laertes' pardon and specifically cites his own abuse of charity: "I have shot my arrow o'er the house/And hurt my brother" (Act V, Sc. 2). His professed love of Ophelia has not exhibited charity, nor has his interview with his mother.

Style

Methods of Analyzing Style

When we address ourselves to the problems of style, we are, in effect, addressing ourselves to a relatively large group of components rather than to a single entity. Style is the basic verbal presentation of ideas and, in particular, the ways in which one specified author or dramatist *chooses* to express his ideas. Under the heading of style we place such components as arrangement, diction, rhythm, emphasis, figurative language, imagery, abstractions, etc. The best place to begin, it would seem, is with a consideration of diction.

1. Diction

Diction is the choice of words in expressing ideas. The words themselves constitute what we term a "vocabulary," while diction has to do with how the words of this vocabulary are chosen. In John Knowles' well-known novel, *A Separate Peace,* for example, the diction is military: that is, ideas are expressed in terms of war and the vocabulary of war is employed. In *Macbeth,* there is a great deal of the vocabulary of witchcraft and many of the ideas are presented in terms suggestive of mystery and horror. Diction refers only to the selection of the words; the manner in which the author arranges them constitutes the essence of his particular style.

2. Imagery

In works of art we discover various "images" or representations of objects and people which somehow educate our senses. An image is a figure of speech employed in such a way that something comes to have a greater meaning than is implied in its literal sense. If throughout a play or a poem we find a linking between light and goodness, while at the same time we find an association of evil with darkness, we can then speak of the imagery of light and darkness. If many images of a similar nature are used we can begin to speak of various "patterns of imagery." For example, in Dickens' long novel *Bleak House,* every character is slowly associated with either an animal that is predatory or an animal which is meek and preyed upon. Thus we can speak of the imagery of hunting, or of imprisonment.

3. Figurative Language

An author places his own particular stamp on his work by employing figurative language. That is, the author communicates ideas to us by way of *analogies.* In a certain "figure" the poet presents one thing on the surface while very directly implying something else beneath the surface. The most common figures are the simile and the metaphor. In a simile, the poet or writer says that "X is *like* (or as) Y," while in a metaphor, the poet says "X is Y," in both cases hoping to increase our appreciation for something by showing us something analagous to it. "My love is a rose" is a metaphor which suggests to us the beauty and the developing freshness of love by associating love with a rose. Throughout most works of literature we discover figures of speech and although metaphors and similes are the most common, the student should also acquaint himself with other figures such as "antithesis," "personification," "metonymy," "synecdoche," and "hyperbole."

4. Emphasis

The principle behind "emphasis" is simply that the writer should devote the right amount of attention to what is more important; that is, the time spent on certain ideas should correspond roughly to the importance of those ideas within the work. The sequence of presentation is important, but the main consideration is that the author does not spend a disproportionate amount of time on something trivial or, conversely, insufficient time on what is of major importance. Furthermore, when we consider emphasis as a component of an author's style, we should try to notice how detail is subordinated to the larger ideas.

Put another way, we need to concentrate on the relationship of detail to what is universally implied. This leads us into a consideration of what is *general* and what is *particular*. We should single out some of the major statements of the theme, and then demonstrate their general truth by noting the ways in which particular statements support them.

5. Point of View

One aspect of style not discernible as easily in a play, but often of central importance to the understanding of a novel or a poem, is "point of view." We explain the attitude which the narrator or poet has toward his material. Further, what is the perspective of the poet? Is he writing about something in the past? If so, how far into the past? Is he sad about what happened? In short, by posing a series of questions we try to discover the writer's basic feelings behind the narration of the story; by explaining the position of the narrator we automatically describe the ways in which we can talk about a particular literary work.

6. Subjective Elements of Style

As style concerns the ways in which one particular author offers us a set of ideas, we must explain precisely what is particular about his methods. What are the private and personal feelings which shade all of the material? Is Shakespeare, for example, abnormally hateful of jealousy and is this hatred reflected in his style? Does the author have an anti-feminism which can be seen evidenced in certain stylistic excesses? This leads to a final consideration.

7. Comparing to Style of Other Works by Same Author

Because we are interested primarily in making conclusions about the style of one particular work and not about the author, we should try to discover what is unique about the style of one of his works. By comparing the style of the work with which we are concerned with the style of other works by the same author, we can either make generalizations about the author's style, or else explain what is stylistically unique about the particular work in question.

Questions and Answers on Style

Question 14.

Identify some of the chief characteristics of style in *Hamlet*.

Answer

When *Hamlet* (as we know it) was written, Shakespeare had left behind him those early years of authorship when his plays were rhyming poems and his imagery was mere decoration; he had passed through the period of transition (e.g. *Romeo and Juliet* and *Richard II*) which still showed many marks of immaturity. In *Hamlet* Shakespeare shows himself to be a master craftsman. The early scenes of the play are remarkable for their rapid dialogue in verse, in which the supernatural is realistically brought into contact with the real. The prose, which is used liberally throughout the play, contains several masterful pieces of rhetoric. The soliloquies are excellent examples of slow, contemplative verse, and are very appropriate to the expression of thought in solitude. Like other plays by Shakespeare, *Hamlet* is also remarkable for its wealth of imagery, and especially for its use of metaphor. Note, for example, Act III, Sc. 3, 11-23, where three successive images express the same thought, and Act III, Sc. 4, 40-51, where the metaphors "are flaming apparitions, which are like a picture in a flash of lightning."

Question 15.

Discuss Hamlet's language in terms of his use of allusion and imagery.

Answer

In addition to thematic motifs that unify the play, *Hamlet* is integrated by specific allusions and image patterns. Hamlet's keen observation of the world around him is demonstrated in his many references to antiquity, courtier life, falconry, fine arts, military life, natural science and mythology. His intellectuality and intelligence, his social bearing and his interest in contemporary events reflect his character and help us recognize the tension he must experience in pursuing the course of action necessary to revenge. Hamlet's speech, beginning on line 54 of Act III, Sc. 4, reveals his extensive knowledge of mythology. He mentions *Hyperion's curls, the front of Jove himself, An eye like Mars* and *the herald Mercury* in the space of only three lines.

The recurrent image patterns in Hamlet's speech consist of references to disease and decay (representing corruption) and to human parts (emphasizing the animal, not angelic, side of man). In the same speech cited above, Hamlet refers to *a mildew'd ear, Blasting,* sense that is *apoplex'd, madness, a sickly part of one true sense,* and a few lines later, *rank sweat,* an *enseamed bed* and *Stewed in corruption.* Images relating to parts of the body are contained in references to *brow, curls, front, bones, eyes* (four times), and *ears.* Notice also the language of Claudius' prayer in Act III, Sc. 3, 36-71: *rank, smells, corrupted, wretched state, black as death, limed soul; hand, blood, teeth, forehead, bosom, knees, heart* and *sinews.* The pattern of disease and decay evoked in both Hamlet's and Claudius' speeches correlates with the rottenness of the state (of which these two characters are most consciously aware), the deceit and faithlessness underlying the action, and the multiple deaths. The pattern of human parts, on the other hand, points to the theme of man and his nature.

Question 16.
Account for the use of prose throughout so much of Act III, Scene 2, which deals largely with the arrival and performance of the players.

Answer
It has been commented earlier (See Shakespeare's Artistry) that the usual vehicle of Shakespeare's plays is iambic pentameter verse, unrhymed or 'blank.' Prose is used to denote a change in, usually a lowering of, dramatic pitch, a character speaking out of his natural part, outside matter (such as letters), and the speeches of characters of lower social rank.

In this act, most of the prose is of a higher character than that used elsewhere to provide comic relief. In the early part of the act, the use of prose shows the contrast between Hamlet when he is his natural self and Hamlet when he has assumed the appearance of madness. In conversation with Rosencrantz and Guildenstern, there is a contrast between Hamlet the fellow-student and Hamlet the prince. In conversation with the Players, there may be two reasons for the use of prose: to mark the degree of familiarity that exists between Hamlet and his old friend, and to strengthen the contrast between the dramatic play of *Hamlet* and the epic tragedy of Gonzago.

It should be noted, however, that some of the prose of this act, such as Hamlet's speech regarding "What a piece of work is a man," is very highly crafted and is more full of concentrated meaning than almost any of the blank verse of the play.

Question 17.
Cite examples from this drama of plays on words (puns).

Answer
Of the numerous examples of puns that are to be found in this play, the following are some of the most obvious:
1. On *kin* and *kind* (Act I, Sc. 2).
2. On three meanings of *tender* (Act I, Sc. 3).
3. On *Capitol* and *capital, Brutus* and *Brute* (Act III, Sc. 2).
4. On two meanings of *fret* (Act III, Sc. 2).
5. On the different meanings of *fine* (Act V, Sc. 1).
6. On two meanings of *assurance* (Act V, Sc. 1).
7. On two meanings of *lie* and *quick* (Act V, Sc. 1).
8. On two meanings of *ground* (Act V, Sc. 1).
9. On two meanings of *foil* (Act V, Sc. 2).

Question 18.
Discuss the poetic merits of Hamlet's soliloquy in Act II, Scene 2, which begins "O, what a rogue and peasant slave am I."

Answer

This soliloquy is in iambic pentameter blank (unrhymed) verse whose language is personal and direct, giving an effect of unrehearsed spontaneity. The poetic merits are many and varied, but two stand out: the effective imagery ("murder, though it hath no tongue, will speak/ With most miraculous organ") in which the crime, murder, is personified, and alliteration of the m - sounds sustains the effect; and the dramatic intermingling of the *two* voices of Hamlet, that of the calm, reasonable aristocrat (as in "O, what a rogue and peasant slave am I!") contrasted with that of the passionate, disturbed man (as in "this slave's offal;"). Hamlet realizes that he has been speaking out of character when he accuses himself of having had to

> unpack my heart with words,
> And fall a cursing, like a very drab.
> A scullion.

This intermixing by Shakespeare of courtly vocabulary and syntax with household cursing, in a single soliloquy, is a very effective poetic device, because it reveals Hamlet's mind working at at least two levels when trying to resolve his tragic conflict.

*The World of *Hamlet*

My subject is the world of *Hamlet*. I do not of course mean Denmark, except as Denmark is given a body by the play; and I do not mean Elizabethan England, though this is necessarily close behind the scenes. I mean simply the imaginative environment that the play asks us to enter when we read it or go to see it.

Great plays, as we know, do present us with something that can be called a world, a microcosm—a world like our own in being made of people, actions, situations, thoughts, feelings, and much more, but unlike our own in being perfectly, or almost perfectly, significant and coherent. In a play's world, each part implies the other parts, and each lives, each means, with the life and meaning of the rest.

This is the reason, as we also know, that the worlds of great plays greatly differ. Othello in Hamlet's position, we sometimes say, would have no problem; but what we are really saying is that Othello in Hamlet's position would not exist. The conception we have of Othello is a function of the characters who help define him, Desdemona, honest Iago, Cassio, and the rest; of his history of travel and war; of a great storm that divides his ship from Cassio's, and a handkerchief; of a quiet night in Venice broken by cries about an old black ram; of a quiet night in Cyprus broken by swordplay; of a quiet bedroom where a

---

*By Maynard Mack. From *The Yale Review,* XLI (1952).

woman goes to bed in her wedding sheets and a man comes in with a light to put out the light; and above all, of a language, a language with many voices in it, gentle, rasping, querulous, or foul, but all counter-pointing the one great voice:

Put up your bright swords, for the dew will rust them. [1]

O thou weed
Who art so lovely fair and smell'st so sweet
That the sense aches at thee. . . . [2]

Yet I'll not shed her blood
Nor scar that whiter skin of hers than snow,
And smooth as monumental alabaster. [3]

I pray you in your letters,
When you shall these unlucky deeds relate,
Speak of me as I am; nothing extenuate,
Nor set down aught in malice; then must you speak
Of one that loved not wisely but too well;
Of one not easily jealous, but being wrought,
Perplex'd in th' extreme; of one whose hand,
Like the base Indian, threw a pearl away
Richer than all his tribe. . . . [4]

Without his particular world of voices, persons, events, the world that both expresses and contains him, Othello is unimaginable. And so, I think, are Antony, King Lear, Macbeth—and Hamlet. We come back then to Hamlet's world, of all the tragic worlds that Shakespeare made, easily the most various and brilliant, the most elusive. It is with no thought of doing justice to it that I have singled out three of its attributes for comment. I know too well, if I may echo a sentiment of Mr. E. M. W. Tillyard's, that no one is likely to accept another man's reading of *Hamlet,* that anyone who tries to throw light on one part of the play usually throws the rest into deeper shadow, and that what I have to say leaves out many problems—to mention only one, the knotty problem of the text. All I would say in defense of the materials I have chosen is that they seem to be interesting, close to the root of the matter even if we continue to differ about what the root of the matter is, and explanatory, in a modest way, of this play's peculiar hold on everyone's imagination, its almost mythic status, one might say, as a paradigm of the life of man.

The first attribute that impresses us, I think, is mysteriousness. We often hear it said, perhaps with truth, that every great work of art has a mystery at the heart; but the mystery of *Hamlet* is something else. We feel its presence in the numberless explanations that have been brought forward for Hamlet's delay, his madness, his ghost, his treatment of Polonius, or Ophelia, or his mother; and in the controversies that still go on about whether the play is "undoubtedly a failure" (Eliot's phrase) or one of the greatest artistic triumphs; whether, if it is a triumph, it belongs to the highest order of tragedy; whether, if it is such a tragedy, its hero is to be taken as a man of exquisite moral sensibility (Bradley's view) or an egomaniac (Madariaga's view).

Doubtless there have been more of these controversies and explanations than the play requires; for in Hamlet, to paraphrase a remark of Falstaff's, we have a character who is not only mad in himself but a cause that madness is in the rest of us. Still, the very existence of so many theories and counter-theories, many of them formulated by sober heads, gives food for thought. *Hamlet* seems to lie closer to the illogical logic of life than Shakespeare's other tragedies. And while the causes of this situation may be sought by saying that Shakespeare revised the play so often that eventually the motivations were smudged over, or that the original old play has been here or there imperfectly digested, or that the problems of Hamlet lay so close to Shakespeare's heart that he could not quite distance them in the formal terms of art, we have still as critics to deal with effects, not causes. If I may quote again from Mr. Tillyard, the play's very lack of a rigorous type of causal logic seems to be a part of its point.

Moreover, the matter goes deeper than this. Hamlet's world is pre-eminently in the interrogative mood. It reverberates with questions, anguished, meditative, alarmed. There are questions that in this play, to an extent I think unparalleled in any other, mark the phases and even the nuances of the action, helping to establish its peculiar baffled tone. There are other questions whose interrogations, innocent at first glance, are subsequently seen to have reached beyond their contexts and to point towards some pervasive inscrutability in Hamlet's world as a whole. Such is that tense series of challenges with which the tragedy begins: Bernardo's of Francisco, "Who's there?" Francisco's of Horatio and Marcellus, "Who is there?" Horatio's of the ghost, "What art thou . . . ?" And then there are the famous questions. In them the interrogations seem to point not only beyond the context but beyond the play, out of Hamlet's predicaments into everyone's: "What a piece of work is a man! . . . And yet to me what is this quintessence of dust?" "To be, or not to be, that is the question." "Get thee to a nunnery. Why wouldst thou be a breeder of sinners?" "I am very proud, revengeful, ambitious, with more offences at my beck than I have thoughts to put them in, imagination to give them shape, or time to act them in. What should such fellows as I do crawling between earth and heaven?" "Dost thou think Alexander look'd o' this fashion i' th' earth? . . . And smelt so?"

Further, Hamlet's world is a world of riddles. The hero's own language is often riddling, as the critics have pointed out. When he puns, his puns have receding depths in them, like the one which constitutes his first speech: "A little more than kin, and less than kind." His utterances in madness, even if wild and whirling, are simultaneously, as Polonius discovers, pregnant: "Do you know me, my lord?" "Excellent well. You are a fishmonger." Even the madness itself is riddling: How much is real? How much is feigned? What does it mean? Sane or mad, Hamlet's mind plays restlessly about his world, turning up one riddle upon another. The riddle of character, for example, and how it is that in a man whose virtues else are "pure as grace," some vicious mole of nature, some "dram of eale," can "all the noble substance oft adulter." Or the riddle of the player's art, and how a man can so project himself into a fiction, a dream of passion, that he can weep for Hecuba. Or the riddle of action: how we may think too little—"What to ourselves in passion we propose," says the player-king, "The passion ending, doth the purpose lose;" and again, how we may think too much: "Thus conscience does make cowards of us all, And thus the native hue of resolution Is sicklied o'er with the pale cast of thought."

There are also more immediate riddles. His mother—how could she "on this fair mountain leave to feed, And batten on this moor?" The ghost—which may be a devil, for "the de'il hath power T' assume a pleasing shape." Ophelia—what does her behavior to him mean? Surprising her in her closet, he falls to such perusal of her face as he would draw it. Even the king at his prayers is a riddle. Will a revenge that takes him in the purging of his soul be vengeance, or hire and salary? As for himself, Hamlet realizes, he is the greatest riddle of all—a mystery, he warns Rosencrantz and Guildenstern, from which he will not have the heart plucked out. He cannot tell why he has of late lost all his mirth, forgone all custom of exercises. Still less can he tell why he delays: "I do not know Why yet I live to say, 'This thing's to do,' Sith I have cause and will and strength and means To do 't."

Thus the mysteriousness of Hamlet's world is of a piece. It is not simply a matter of missing motivations, to be expunged if only we could find the perfect clue. It is built in. It is evidently an important part of what the play wishes to say to us. And it is certainly an element that the play thrusts upon us from the opening word. Everyone, I think, recalls the mysteriousness of that first scene. The cold middle of the night on the castle platform, the muffled sentries, the uneasy atmosphere of apprehension, the challenges leaping out of the dark, the questions that follow the challenges, feeling out the darkness, searching for identities, for relations, for assurance. "Bernardo?" "Have you had quiet guard?" "Who hath reliev'd you?" "What, is Horatio there?" "What, has this thing appear'd again tonight?" "Looks 'a not like the king?" "How now, Horatio! . . . Is not this something more than fantasy? What think you on 't?" "It is not like the king?" "Why this same strict and most observant watch . . . ?" "Shall I strike at it with my partisan?" "Do you consent we shall acquaint [young Hamlet] with it?"

We need not be surprised that critics and playgoers alike have been tempted to see in this an evocation not simply of Hamlet's world but of their own. Man in his aspect of bafflement, moving in darkness on a rampart between two worlds, unable to reject, or quite accept, the one that, when he faces it, "to-shakes" his disposition with thoughts beyond the reaches of his soul—comforting himself with hints and guesses. We hear these hints and guesses whispering through the darkness as the several watchers speak. "At least, the whisper goes so," says one. "I think it be no other but e'en so," says another. "I have heard" that on the crowing of the cock "Th' extravagant and erring spirit hies To his confine," says a third. "Some say" at Christmas time "this bird of dawning" sings all night, "And then, they say, no spirit dare stir abroad." "So have I heard," says the first, "and do in part believe it." However we choose to take the scene, it is clear that it creates a world where uncertainties are of the essence.

Meantime, such is Shakespeare's economy, a second attribute of Hamlet's world has been put before us. This is the problematic nature of reality and the relation of reality to appearance. The play begins with an appearance, an "apparition," to use Marcellus's term—the ghost. And the ghost is somehow real, indeed the vehicle of realities. Through its revelation, the glittering surface of Claudius's court is pierced, and Hamlet comes to know, and we do, that the king is not only hateful to him but the murderer of his father, that his mother is guilty of adultery as well as incest. Yet there is a dilemma in the revelation. For possibly the apparition *is* an apparition, a devil who has assumed his father's shape.

This dilemma, once established, recurs on every hand. From the court's point of view, there is Hamlet's madness. Polonius investigates and gets some strange advice about his daughter: "Conception is a blessing, but as your daughter may conceive, friend, look to 't." Rosencrantz and Guildenstern investigate and get the strange confidence that "Man delights not me; no, nor woman neither." Ophelia is "loosed" to Hamlet (Polonius's vulgar word), while Polonius and the king hide behind the arras; and what they hear is a strange indictment of human nature, and a riddling threat: "Those that are married already, all but one, shall live."

On the other hand, from Hamlet's point of view, there is Ophelia. Kneeling here at her prayers, she seems the image of innocence and devotion. Yet she is of the sex for whom he has already found the name Frailty, and she is also, as he seems either madly or sanely to divine, a decoy in a trick. The famous cry—"Get thee to a nunnery"—shows the anguish of his uncertainty. If Ophelia is what she seems, this dirty-minded world of murder, incest, lust, adultery, is no place for her. Were she "as chaste as ice, as pure as snow," she could not escape its calumny. And if she is not what she seems, then a nunnery in its other sense of brothel is relevant to her. In the scene that follows he treats her as if she were indeed an inmate of a brothel.

Likewise, from Hamlet's point of view, there is the enigma of the king. If the ghost is *only* an appearance, then possibly the king's appearance is reality. He must try it further. By means of a second and different kind of "apparition," the play within the play, he does so. But then, immediately after, he stumbles on the king at prayer. This appearance has a relish of salvation in it. If the king dies now, his soul may yet be saved. Yet actually, as we know, the king's efforts to come to terms with heaven have been unavailing; his words fly up, his thoughts remain below. If Hamlet means the conventional revenger's reasons that he gives for sparing Claudius, it was the perfect moment not to spare him—when the sinner was acknowledging his guilt, yet unrepentant. The perfect moment, but it was hidden, like so much else in the play, behind an arras.

There are two arrases in his mother's room. Hamlet thrusts his sword through one of them. Now at last he has got to the heart of the evil, or so he thinks. But now it is the wrong man; now he himself is a murderer. The other arras he stabs through with his words—like daggers, says the queen. He makes her shrink under the contrast he points between her present husband and his father. But as the play now stands (matters are somewhat clearer in the bad Quarto), it is hard to be sure how far the queen grasps the fact that her second husband is the murderer of her first. And it is hard to say what may be signified by her inability to see the ghost, who now for the last time appears. In one sense at least, the ghost is the supreme reality, representative of the hidden ultimate power, in Bradley's terms—witnessing from beyond the grave against this hollow world. Yet the man who is capable of seeing through to this reality, the queen thinks is mad. "To whom do you speak this?" she cries to her son. "Do you see nothing there?" he asks, incredulous. And she replies: "Nothing at all; yet all that is I see." Here certainly we have the imperturbable self-confidence of the worldly world, its layers on layers of habituation, so that when the reality is before its very eyes it cannot detect its presence.

Like mystery, this problem of reality is central to the play and written deep into its idiom. Shakespeare's favorite terms in *Hamlet* are words of ordinary usage that pose the question of appearances in a fundamental form. "Apparition" I have already mentioned. Another term is "seems." When we say, as Ophelia says of Hamlet leaving her closet. "He seem'd to find his way without his eyes," we mean one thing. When we say, as Hamlet says to his mother in the first court-scene, "Seems, Madam! . . . I know not 'seems,'" we mean another. And when we say, as Hamlet says to Horatio before the play within the play, "And after, we will both our judgments join In censure of his seeming," we mean both at once. The ambiguities of "seem" coil and uncoil throughout this play, and over against them is set the idea of "seeing." So Hamlet challenges the king in his triumphant letter announcing his return to Denmark: "Tomorrow shall I beg leave to see your kingly eyes." Yet "seeing" itself can be ambiguous, as we recognize from Hamlet's uncertainty about the ghost; or from that statement of his mother's already quoted: "Nothing at all; yet all that is I see."

Another term of like importance is "assume." What we assume may be what we are not: "The de'il hath power T' assume a pleasing shape." But it may be what we are: "If it assume my noble father's person, I'll speak to it." And it may be what we are not yet, but would become; thus Hamlet advises his mother, "Assume a virtue, if you have it not." The perplexity in the word points to a real perplexity in Hamlet's and our own experience. We assume our habits—and habits are like costumes, as the word implies: "My father in his habit as he liv'd!" Yet these habits become ourselves in time: "That monster, custom, who all sense doth eat Of habits evil, is angel yet in this, That to the use of actions fair and good He likewise gives a frock or livery That aply is put on."

Two other terms I wish to instance are "put on" and "shape." The shape of something is the form under which we are accustomed to apprehend it: "Do you see yonder cloud that's almost in shape of a camel?" But a shape may also be a disguise—even, in Shakespeare's time, an actor's costume or an actor's role. This is the meaning when the king says to Laertes as they lay the plot against Hamlet's life: "Weigh that convenience both of time and means May fit us to our shape." "Put on" supplies an analogous ambiguity. Shakespeare's mind seems to worry this phrase in the play much as Hamlet's mind worries the problem of acting in a world of surfaces, or the king's mind worries the meaning of Hamlet's transformation. Hamlet has put an antic disposition on, that the king knows. But what does "put on" mean? A mask, or a frock or livery—our "habit"? The king is left guessing, and so are we.

What is found in the play's key terms is also found in its imagery. Miss Spurgeon has called attention to a pattern of disease images in *Hamlet,* to which I shall return. But the play has other patterns equally striking. One of these, as my earlier quotations hint, is based on clothes. In the world of surfaces to which Shakespeare exposes us in Hamlet, clothes are naturally a factor of importance. "The apparel oft proclaims the man," Polonius assures Laertes, cataloguing maxims in the young man's ear as he is about to leave for Paris. Oft, but not always. And so he sends his man Reynaldo to look into Laertes' life there—even, if need be, to put a false dress of accusation upon his son ("What forgeries you please"), the better by indirections to find directions out. On the same grounds, he takes Hamlet's vows to Ophelia a false apparel. They are bawds, he tells her—or if we do not like Theobald's emendation, they are bonds—in masquerade, "Not of that dye which their investments show, But mere implorators of unholy suits."

This breach between the outer and the inner stirs no special emotion in Polonius, because he is always either behind an arras or prying into one, but it shakes Hamlet to the core. Here so recently was his mother in her widow's weeds, the tears still flushing in her galled eyes; yet now within a month, a little month, before even her funeral shoes are old, she has married with his uncle. Her mourning was all clothes. Not so his own, he bitterly replies, when she asks him to cast his "nighted color off." "Tis not alone my inky cloak, good mother"—and not alone, he adds, the sighs, the tears, the dejected havior of the visage—"that can denote me truly."

> These indeed seem,
> For they are actions that a man might play;
> But I have that within which passes show;
> These but the trappings and the suits of woe.[5]

What we must not overlook here is Hamlet's visible attire, giving the verbal imagery a theatrical extension. Hamlet's apparel now is his inky cloak, mark of his grief for his father, mark also of his character as a man of melancholy, mark possibly too of his being one in whom appearance and reality are attuned. Later, in his madness, with his mind disordered, he will wear his costume in a corresponding disarray, the disarray that Ophelia describes so vividly to Polonius and that producers of the play rarely give sufficient heed to: "Lord Hamlet with his doublet all unbrac'd, No hat upon his head; his stockings foul'd, Ungarter'd, and down-gyved to his ankle." Here the only question will be, as with the madness itself, how much is studied, how much is real. Still later, by a third costume, the simple traveler's garb in which we find him new come from shipboard. Shakespeare will show us that we have a third aspect of the man.

A second pattern of imagery springs from terms of painting: the paints, the colorings, the varnishes that may either conceal or, as in the painter's art, reveal. Art in Claudius conceals. "The harlot's cheek," he tells us in his one aside, "beautied with plastering art, Is not more ugly to the thing that helps it Than is my deed to my most painted word." Art in Ophelia, loosed to Hamlet in the episode already noticed to which this speech of the king's is prelude, is more complex. She looks so beautiful—"the celestial, and my soul's idol, the most beautified Ophelia," Hamlet has called her in his love letter. But now, what does beautified mean? Perfected with all the innocent beauties of a lovely woman? Or "beautied" like the harlot's cheek? "I have heard of your paintings too, well enough. God hath given you one face, and you make yourselves another."

Yet art, differently used, may serve the truth. By using an

"image" (his own word) of a murder done in Vienna, Hamlet cuts through to the king's guilt; holds "as 'twere, the mirror up to nature," shows "virtue her own feature, scorn her own image, and the very age and body of the time"—which is out of joint—"his form and pressure." Something similar he does again in his mother's bedroom, painting for her in words "the rank sweat of an enseamed bed," making her recoil in horror from his "counterfeit presentment of two brothers," and holding, if we may trust a stage tradition, his father's picture beside his uncle's. Here again the verbal imagery is realized visually on the stage.

The most pervasive of Shakespeare's image patterns in this play, however, is the pattern evolved around the three words, show, act, play. "Show" seems to be Shakespeare's unifying image in *Hamlet*. Through it he pulls together and exhibits in a single focus much of the diverse material in his play. The ideas of seeming, assuming, and putting on; the images of clothing, painting, mirroring; the episode of the dumb show and the play within the play; the characters of Polonius, Laertes, Ophelia, Claudius, Gertrude, Rosencrantz and Guildenstern, Hamlet himself—all these at one time or another, and usually more than once, are drawn into the range of implications flung round the play by "show."

"Act," on the other hand, I take to be the play's radical metaphor. It distills the various perplexities about the character of reality into a residual perplexity about the character of an act. What, this play asks again and again, is an act? What is its relation to the inner act, the intent? "If I drown myself wittingly," says the clown in the graveyard, "it argues an act, and an act hath three branches; it is to act, to do, to perform." Or again, the play asks, how does action relate to passion, that "laps'd in time and passion" I can let "go by Th' important acting of your dread command"; and to thought, which can so sickly o'er the native hue of resolution that "enterprises of great pitch and moment With this regard their currents turn awry, And lose the name of action"; and to words, which are not acts, and so we dare not be content to unpack our hearts with them, and yet are acts of a sort, for we may speak daggers though we use none. Or still again, how does an act (a deed) relate to an act (a pretense)? For an action may be nothing but pretense. So Polonius readying Ophelia for the interview with Hamlet, with "pious action," as he phrases it, "sugar[s] o'er The devil himself." Or it may not be a pretense, yet not what it appears. So Hamlet spares the king, finding him in an act that has some "relish of salvation in 't." Or it may be a pretense that is also the first foothold of a new reality, as when we assume a virtue though we have it not. Or it may be a pretense that is actually a mirroring of reality, like the play within the play, or the tragedy of *Hamlet*.

To this network of implications, the third term, play, adds an additional dimension. "Play" is a more precise word, in Elizabethan parlance at least, for all the elements in *Hamlet* that pertain to the art of the theatre; and it extends their field of reference till we see that every major personage in the tragedy is a player in some sense, and every major episode a play. The court plays, Hamlet plays, the players play, Rosencrantz and Guildenstern try to play on Hamlet, though they cannot play on his recorders—here we have an extension to a musical sense. And the final duel, by a further extension, becomes itself a play, in which everyone but Claudius and Laertes plays his role in ignorance: "The queen desires you to show some gentle entertainment to Laertes before you fall to play." "I . . . will this brother's wager frankly play." "Give him the cup."—"I'll play this bout first."

The full extension of this theme is best evidenced in the play within the play itself. Here, in the bodily presence of these traveling players, bringing with them the latest playhouse gossip out of London, we have suddenly a situation that tends to dissolve the normal barriers between the fictive and the real. For here on the stage before us is a play of false appearances in which an actor called the player-king is playing. But there is also on the stage, Claudius, another player-king, who is a spectator of this player. And there is on the stage, besides, a prince who is a spectator of both these player-kings and who plays with great intensity a player's role himself. And around these kings and that prince is a group of courtly spectators—Gertrude, Rosencrantz, Guildenstern, Polonius, and the rest—and they, as we have come to know, are players too. And lastly there are ourselves, an audience watching all these audiences who are also players. Where, it may suddenly occur to us to ask, does the playing end? Which *are* the guilty creatures sitting at a play? When is an act not an "act"?

The mysteriousness of Hamlet's world, while it pervades the tragedy, finds its point of greatest dramatic concentration in the first act, and its symbol in the first scene. The problems of appearance and reality also pervade the play as a whole, but come to a climax in Acts II and III, and possibly their best symbol is the play within the play. Our third attribute, though again it is one that crops out everywhere, reaches its full development in Acts IV and V. It is not easy to find an appropriate name for this attribute, but perhaps "mortality" will serve, if we remember to mean by mortality the heartache and the thousand natural shocks that flesh is heir to, not simply death.

The powerful sense of mortality in *Hamlet* is conveyed to us, I think, in three ways. First, there is the play's emphasis on human weakness, the instability of human purpose, the subjection of humanity to fortune—all that we might call the aspect of failure in man. Hamlet opens this theme in Act I, when he describes how from that single blemish, perhaps not even the victim's fault, a man's whole character may take corruption. Claudius dwells on it again, to an extent that goes far beyond the needs of the occasion, while engaged in seducing Laertes to step behind the arras of a seemer's world and dispose of Hamlet by a trick. Time qualifies everything, Claudius says, including love, including purpose. As for love—it has a "plurisy" in it and dies of its own too much. As for purpose—"That we would do, We should do when we would, for this 'would' changes, And hath abatements and delays as many As there are tongues, are hands, are accidents; And then this 'should' is like a spendthrift's sigh, That hurts by easing." The player-king, in his long speeches to his queen in the play within the play, sets the matter in a still darker light. She means these protestations of undying love, he knows, but our purposes depend on our memory, and our memory fades fast. Or else, he suggests, we propose something to ourselves in a condition of strong feeling, but then the feeling goes, and with it the resolve. Or else our fortunes change, he adds, and with these our loves: "The great man down, you mark his favorite flies." The subjection of human aims to fortune is a reiterated theme in *Hamlet*, as subsequently in *Lear*. Fortune is the harlot goddess in whose secret parts men like Rosencrantz and Guildenstern live and thrive; the strumpet who threw down Troy and Hecuba and Priam; the outrageous foe whose slings and arrows a man of principle must suffer or seek release in suicide. Horatio suffers them with composure: he is one of the blessed few "Whose blood and judgment are so well co-mingled That they are not a pipe for fortune's finger To sound what stop she please." For Hamlet the task is of a greater difficulty.

Next, and intimately related to this matter of infirmity, is the emphasis on infection—the ulcer, the hidden abscess, "th' imposthume of much wealth and peace That inward breaks and shows no cause without Why the man dies." Miss Spurgeon, who was the first to call attention to this aspect of the play, has well remarked that so far as Shakespeare's pictorial imagination is concerned, the problem in *Hamlet* is not a problem of the will and reason, "of a mind too philosophical or a nature temperamentally unfitted to act quickly," nor even a problem of an individual at all. Rather, it is a condition—"a condition for which the individual himself is apparently not responsible, any more than the sick man is to blame for the infection which strikes and devours him, but which, nevertheless, in its course and development, impartially and relentlessly, annihilates him and others, innocent and guilty alike." "That," she adds, "is the tragedy of *Hamlet*, as it is perhaps the chief tragic mystery of life." This is a perceptive comment, for it reminds us that Hamlet's situation is mainly not of his own manufacture, as are the situations of Shakespeare's other tragic heroes. He has inherited it; he is "born to set it right."

We must not, however, neglect to add to this what another student of Shakespeare's imagery has noticed—that the infection in Denmark is presented alternatively as poison. Here, of course, responsibility is implied, for the poisoner of the play is Claudius. The juice he pours into the ear of the elder Hamlet is a combined poison and disease, a "leperous distilment" that curds "the thin and wholesome blood." From this fatal center, unwholesomeness spreads out till there is something rotten in all Denmark. Hamlet tells us that his "wit's diseased," the queen speaks of her "sick soul," the king is troubled by "the hectic" in his blood, Laertes meditates revenge to warm "the sickness in my heart," the people of the kingdom grow "muddied, Thick and unwholesome in their thoughts"; and even Ophelia's madness is said to be "the poison of deep grief." In the end, all save Ophelia die of that poison in a literal as well as figurative sense.

But the chief form in which the theme of mortality reaches us, it seems to me, is as a profound consciousness of loss. Hamlet's father expresses something of the kind when he tells Hamlet how his "most seeming-virtuous queen," betraying a love which "was of that dignity That it went hand in hand even with the vow I made to her in marriage," had chosen to "decline Upon a wretch whose natural gifts were poor To those of mine." "O Hamlet, what a falling off was there!" Ophelia expresses it again, on hearing Hamlet's denunciation of love and woman in the nunnery scene, which she takes to be the product of a disordered brain:

> O what a noble mind is here o'erthrown!
> The courtier's, soldier's, scholar's, eye, tongue, sword;
> Th' expectancy and rose of the fair state,
> The glass of fashion and the mould of form,
> Th' observ'd of all observers, quite, quite down![6]

The passage invites us to remember that we have never actually seen such a Hamlet—that his mother's marriage has brought a falling off in him before we meet him. And then there is that further falling off, if I may call it so, when Ophelia too goes mad—"Divided from herself and her fair judgment, Without the which we are pictures, or mere beasts."

Time was, the play keeps reminding us, when Denmark was a different place. That was before Hamlet's mother took off "the rose From the fair forehead of an innocent love" and set a blister there. Hamlet then was still "th' expectancy and rose of the fair state"; Ophelia, the "rose of May." For Denmark was a garden then, when his father ruled. There had been something heroic about his father—a king who met the threats to Denmark in open battle, fought with Norway, smote the sledded Polacks on the ice, slew the elder Fortinbras in an honorable trial of strength. There had been something godlike about his father too: "Hyperion's curls, the front of Jove himself, An eye like Mars . . . , A station like the herald Mercury." But, the ghost reveals, a serpent was in the garden, and "the serpent that did sting thy father's life Now wears his crown." The martial virtues are put by now. The threats to Denmark are attended to by policy, by agents working deviously for and through an uncle. The moral virtues are put by too. Hyperion's throne is occupied by "a vice of kings," "a king of shreds and patches"; Hyperion's bed, by a satyr, a paddock, a bat, a gib, a bloat king with reechy kisses. The garden is unweeded now, and "grows to seed; things rank and gross in nature Possess it merely." Even in himself he feels the taint, the taint of being his mother's son; and that other taint, from an earlier garden, of which he admonishes Ophelia: "Our virtue cannot so inoculate our old stock but we shall relish of it." "Why wouldst thou be a breeder of sinners?" "What should such fellows as I do crawling between earth and heaven?"

"Hamlet is painfully aware," says Professor Tillyard, "of the baffling human predicament between the angels and the beasts, between the glory of having been made in God's image and the incrimination of being descended from fallen Adam." To this we may add, I think, that Hamlet is more than aware of it; he exemplifies it; and it is for this reason that his problem appeals to us so powerfully as an image of our own.

Hamlet's problem, in its crudest form, is simply the problem of the avenger; he must carry out the injunction of the ghost and kill the king. But this problem, as I ventured to suggest at the outset, is presented in terms of a certain kind of world. The ghost's injunction to act becomes so inextricably bound up for Hamlet with the character of the world in which the action must be taken—its mysteriousness, its baffling appearances, its deep consciousness of infection, frailty, and loss —that he cannot come to terms with either without coming to terms with both.

When we first see him in the play, he is clearly a very young man, sensitive and idealistic, suffering the first shock of growing up. He has taken the garden at face value, we might say, supposing mankind to be only a little lower than the angels. Now in his mother's hasty and incestuous marriage, he discovers evidence of something else, something bestial—though even a beast, he thinks, would have mourned longer. Then comes the revelation of the ghost, bringing a second shock. Not so much because he now knows that his serpent-uncle killed his father; his prophetic soul had almost suspected this. Not entirely, even, because he knows now how far below the angels humanity has fallen in his mother, and how lust—these were the ghost's words—"though to a radiant angel link'd Will sate itself in a celestial bed, And prey on garbage." Rather, because he now sees everywhere, but especially in his own nature, the general taint, taking from life its meaning, from woman her integrity, from the will its strength, turning reason into madness. "Why wouldst thou be a breeder of sinners?" "What should such fellows as I do crawling between earth and heaven?" Hamlet is not the first young man to have felt the heavy and the weary weight of all this unintelligible word; and, like the others, he must come to terms with it.

The ghost's injunction to revenge unfolds a different facet of his problem. The young man growing up is not to be allowed simply to endure a rotten world, he must also act in it. Yet how to begin, among so many enigmatic surfaces? Even Claudius, whom he now knows to be the core of the ulcer, has a plausible exterior. And around Claudius, swathing the evil out of sight, he encounters all those other exteriors, as we have seen. Some of them already deeply infected beneath, like his mother. Some noble, but marked for infection, like Laertes. Some not particularly corrupt but infinitely corruptible, like Rosencrantz and Guildenstern; some mostly weak and foolish like Polonius and Osric. Some, like Ophelia, innocent, yet in their innocence still serving to "skin and film the ulcerous place."

And this is not all. The act required of him, through retributive justice, is one that necessarily involves the doer in the general guilt. Not only because it involves a killing; but because to get at the world of seeming one sometimes has to use its weapons. He himself, before he finishes, has become a player, has put an antic disposition on, has killed a man—the wrong man—has helped drive Ophelia mad, and has sent two friends of his youth to death, mining below their mines, and hoisting the engineer with his own petard. He had never meant to dirty himself with these things, but from the moment of the ghost's challenge to act, this dirtying was inevitable. It is the condition of living at all in such a world. To quote Polonius, who knew that world so well, men become "a little soil'd i' th' working." Here is another matter with which Hamlet has to come to terms.

Human infirmity—all that I have discussed with reference to instability, infection, loss—supplies the problem with its third phase. Hamlet has not only to accept the mystery of man's condition between the angels and the brutes, and not only to act in a perplexing and soiling world. He has also to act within the human limits—"with shabby equipment always deteriorating," if I may adapt some phrases from Eliot's "East Coker," "In the general mess of imprecision of feeling, Undisciplined squads of emotion." Hamlet is aware of that fine poise of body and mind, feeling and thought, that suits the action to the word, the word to the action; that acquires and begets a temperance in the very torrent, tempest, and whirlwind of passion; but he cannot at first achieve it in himself. He vacillates between undisciplined squads of emotion and thinking too precisely on the event. He learns to his cost how easily action can be lost in "acting," and loses it there for a time himself. But these again are only the terms of every man's life. As Anatole France reminds us in a now famous apostrophe to Hamlet: "What one of us thinks without contradiction and acts without incoherence? What one of us is not mad? What one of us does not say with a mixture of pity, comradeship, admiration, and horror, Goodnight, sweet Prince!''

In the last act of the play (or so it seems to me, for I know there can be differences on this point), Hamlet accepts his world and we discover a different man. Shakespeare does not outline for us the process of acceptance any more than he had done with Romeo or was to do with Othello. But he leads us strongly to expect an altered Hamlet, and then, in my opinion, provides him. We must recall that at this point Hamlet has been absent from the stage during several scenes, and that such absences in Shakespearean tragedy usually warn us to be on the watch for a new phase in the development of the character. It is so when we leave King Lear in Gloucester's farmhouse and find him again in Dover fields. It is so when we leave Macbeth at the witches' cave and rejoin him at Dunsinane, hearing of the armies that beset it. Furthermore, and this is an important matter in the theatre—especially important in a play in which the symbolism of clothing has figured largely— Hamlet now looks different. He is wearing a different dress—probably, as Granville-Barker, thinks, his "sea-gown scarf'd" about him, but in any case no longer the disordered costume of his antic disposition. The effect is not entirely dissimilar to that in *Lear*, when the old king wakes out of his madness to find fresh garments on him.

Still more important, Hamlet displays a considerable change of mood. This is not a matter of the way we take the passage about defying augury, as Mr. Tillyard among others seems to think. It is a matter of Hamlet's whole deportment, in which I feel we may legitimately see the deportment of a man who has been "illuminated" in the tragic sense. Bradley's term for it is fatalism, but if this is what we wish to call it, we must at least acknowledge that it is fatalism of a very distinctive kind—a kind that Shakespeare has been willing to touch with the associations of the saying in St. Matthew about the fall of a sparrow, and with Hamlet's recognition that a divinity shapes our ends. The point is not that Hamlet has suddenly become religious; he has been religious all through the play. The point is that he has now learned, and accepted, the boundaries in which human action, human judgment, are enclosed.

Till his return from the voyage he had been trying to act beyond these, had been encroaching on the role of providence, if I may exaggerate to make a vital point. He had been too quick to take the burden of the whole world and its condition upon his limited and finite self. Faced with a task of sufficient difficulty in its own right, he had dilated it into a cosmic problem—as indeed every task is, but if we think about this too precisely we cannot act at all. The whole time is out of joint, he feels, and in his young man's egocentricity, he will set it right. Hence he misjudges Ophelia, seeing in her only a breeder of sinners. Hence he misjudges himself, seeing himself a vermin crawling between earth and heaven. Hence he takes it upon himself to be his mother's conscience, though the ghost has warned that this is no fit task for him, and returns to repeat the warning: "Leave her to heaven, And to those thorns that in her bosom lodge." Even with the king, Hamlet has sought to play at God. *He* it must be who decides the issue of Claudius's salvation, saving him for a more damnable occasion. Now, he has learned that there are limits to the before and after that human reason can comprehend. Rashness, even, is sometimes good. Through rashness he has saved his life from the commission for his death, "and prais'd be rashness for it." This happy circumstance and the unexpected arrival of the pirate ship make it plain that the roles of life are not entirely self-assigned. "There is a divinity that shapes our ends, Rough-hew them how we will." Hamlet is ready now for what may happen, seeking neither to foreknow it nor avoid it. "If it be now, 'tis not to come; if it be not to come, it will be now; if it be not now, yet it will come: the readiness is all."

The crucial evidence of Hamlet's new frame of mind, as I understand it, is the graveyard scene. Here, in its ultimate symbol, he confronts, recognizes, and accepts the condition of being man. It is not simply that he now accepts death, though Shakespeare shows him accepting it in ever more poignant forms: first, in the imagined persons of the politician, the courtier, and the lawyer, who laid their little schemes "to circumvent God," as Hamlet puts it, but now lie here; then in Yorick, whom he knew and played with as a child; and then in Ophelia. This last death tears from him a final cry of passion, but the striking contrast between his behavior and Laertes's reveals how deeply he has changed.

Still, it is not the fact of death that invests this scene with its peculiar power. It is instead the haunting mystery of life itself that Hamlet's speeches point to, holding in its inscrutable folds those other mysteries that he has wrestled with so long. These he now knows for what they are, and lays them by. The mystery of evil is present here—for this is after all the universal graveyard, where, as the clown says humorously, he holds up Adam's profession; where the scheming politician, the hollow courtier, the tricky lawyer, the emperor and the clown and the beautiful young maiden, all come together in an emblem of the world; where even, Hamlet murmurs, one might expect to stumble on "Cain's jawbone, that did the first murther." The mystery of reality is here too—for death puts the question, "What is real?" in its irreducible form, and in the end uncovers all appearances: "Is this the fine of his fines and the recovery of his recoveries, to have his fine pat full of fine dirt?" "Now get you to my lady's chamber, and tell her, let her paint an inch thick, to this favor she must come." Or if we need more evidence of this mystery, there is the anger of Laertes at the lack of ceremonial trappings, and the ambiguous character of Ophelia's own death. "Is she to be buried in Christian burial when she wilfully seeks her own salvation?" asks the gravedigger. And last of all, but most pervasive of all, there is the mystery of human limitation. The grotesque nature of man's little joys, his big ambitions. The fact that the man who used to bear us on his back is now a skull that smells; that the noble dust of Alexander somewhere plugs a bung-hole; that "Imperious Caesar, dead and turn'd to clay, Might stop a hole to keep the wind away." Above all, the fact that a pit of clay is "meet" for such a guest as man, as the gravedigger tells us in his song, and yet that, despite all frailties, and limitations, "That skull had a tongue in it and could sing once."

After the graveyard and what it indicates has come to pass in him, we know that Hamlet is ready for the final contest of mighty opposites. He accepts the world as it is, the world as a duel, in which, whether we know it or not, evil holds the poisoned rapier and the poisoned chalice waits; and in which, if we win at all, it costs not less than everything. I think we understand by the close of Shakespeare's *Hamlet* why it is that unlike the other tragic heroes he is given a soldier's rites upon the stage. For as William Butler Yeats once said, "Why should we honor those who die on the field of battle? A man may show as reckless a courage in entering into the abyss of himself."

Notes

1. *Othello,* Act I, Sc. 2, 59.
2. *Ibid,* Act IV, Sc. 2, 67-69.
3. *Ibid,* Act V, Sc. 2, 3-5.
4. *Ibid,* Act V, Sc. 2, 340-48.
5. *Hamlet,* Act I, Sc. 2, 83-86.
6. *Ibid,* Act III, Sc. 1, 150-54.

*Hamlet as Minister and Scourge

When Hamlet is first preparing to leave his mother's chamber after harrowing her to repentance, he turns to the dead body of Polonius:

> For this same lord,
> I do repent; but heaven hath pleas'd it so,
> To punish me with this, and this with me,
> That I must be their scourge and minister.
> I will bestow him, and will answer well
> The death I gave him.
>
> (Act III, Sc. 4, 172-177)

These provocative, if not enigmatic, lines have received comparatively small attention. In my opinion they contain perhaps the clearest analy-

*By Fredson Bowers. From *PMLA,* LXX (1955).

sis Hamlet makes of his predicament, and are therefore worth a scrupulous enquiry.

The Variorum quotes Malone's paraphrase, "To punish me by making me the instrument of this man's death, and to punish this man by my hand." This is surely the literal meaning of the first lines. Going beyond Malone by seeking the nature of Hamlet's punishment, both Dover Wilson and Kittredge agree that "To punish me with this" means, substantially, that Hamlet perceives his secret will be revealed to Claudius, with serious consequences to himself. Kittredge writes, "the King will at once perceive that he killed Polonius by mistake for him, and will take measures accordingly." And Dover Wilson (quoting "This man shall set me packing"): "The death of Polonius has placed Hamlet within the power of the King."

This view is only superficially plausible, and it should not satisfy as offering the complete, or even the true, interpretation. The reason for Heaven's punishment is left unexamined, and no account is taken of the close syntactical relationship between the first statement about the double punishment, and the second, "That I must be their [i.e., Heaven's] scourge and minister."

For a moment let us look at this second statement. Kittredge comes near to the meaning: "heaven's scourge (of punishment) and heaven's agent—minister of divine retribution." This implies a difference between a scourge and a minister, that is, between an instrument of punishment and one of divine retribution; but how retribution differs from punishment is not indicated, nor is the question considered why Hamlet describes himself in both capacities.

In cases of doubt it is always well to work back through the text. "For this same lord, I do repent." In spite of whatever callousness Hamlet exhibits in "Thou wretched, rash, intruding fool, farewell!" and in "I'll lug the guts into the neighbour room," or in "Safely stow'd," his stated repentance must be based on more than merely practical considerations that now the hunt will be up. Although Polonius' folly has been punished by Hamlet, yet an innocent man has been killed, and Hamlet has stained his hands with blood without attaining his main objective. His attempt at revenge has led him to commit a murder which he had never contemplated. A modern audience is less likely to feel the horror of Polonius' death than an Elizabethan, which would have known from the moment the rapier flashed through the arras that Hamlet was thereafter a doomed man. On the Elizabethan stage, blood demanded blood; and at the most only two or three tragic characters who draw blood for private motives survive the denouement, and then only at the expense of a retirement to the cloister for the rest of their lives.[1]

Hamlet, no bloody madman, may well repent that he has killed an innocent person. This mistake does not excuse him. Elizabethan law, like ours, was very clear that if by premeditation one kills, but accidentally mistakes the object and slays the wrong man, the case was still premeditated murder in the first degree, not manslaughter.[2]

Hamlet repents at the personal level, yet adds, "but heaven hath pleas'd it so,/To punish me with this." There are two implications here. First, Hamlet recognizes that his repentance cannot wash the blood from his hands, and that he must accept whatever penalty is in store for him. Second, the "this" with which he is punished is certainly the body of Polonius, and thus the fact of murder, carrying with it the inevitable penalty for blood. To view heaven's punishment as no more than the exposure of Hamlet's intents to Claudius, so that the revenge will thereafter be made more difficult, is a shallow concept which ignores the blood that has just been shed in defiance of divine law. I am concerned that the primary implication be made clear: Hamlet feels that it has pleased Heaven to punish him with the central fact of murder and one that bore no relation to his mission of justice; moreover, that he has killed the wrong man is an essential part of this punishment.

If Heaven's punishment is taken merely as the revelation of Hamlet's secret to Claudius, with all the consequences that are sure to follow, the punishment would have been comparatively mild, for the play-within-a-play had already effectively revealed Hamlet to Claudius, as well as Claudius to Hamlet. If we carefully follow the implications of the action within the setting of the time-scheme, it is clear that immediately following the mousetrap, and before the killing of Polonius, Claudius has seen Hamlet's murderous intents and has set on foot a plot to kill him. When first conceived after the eavesdropping on Hamlet and Ophelia in the nunnery scene, the English voyage was an innocent expedient to get a peculiarly behaving Hamlet out of the country, perhaps to his cure. However, it becomes a murderous scheme immediately after the play-within-a-play when Claudius changes the ceremonious details and plans to send Hamlet away in the same ship with Rosencrantz and Guildenstern, a necessary factor for the altered commission ordering Hamlet's execution in England. No hint is given that Claudius has altered the original commission in the short interval between the Queen's announcement of Polonius' death and the appearance of Hamlet before him for questioning, nor would there have been time. We learn only that Polonius' death must expedite Hamlet's departure; and hence we are required to assume that the discussion of the commission immediately following the mousetrap play involved what we later learn to have been the important change commanding Hamlet's death. Viewed in this light, the dead body of Polonius cannot punish Hamlet by revealing his secret to Claudius, for that has previously been revealed, and Claudius has already set on foot a lethal plot to dispose of his stepson.

Of course, Hamlet does not know of the change in the purport of the commission, it might be argued. But it would be most difficult to argue that Hamlet was not quite aware that in stripping the truth from Claudius by the doctored-up *Murder of Gonzago,* he had simultaneously revealed himself. The circumstances and language of the play were too damning for him to think that more than the façade of pretense could stand between him and Claudius after that episode. Hence I take it that the conventional interpretation of Hamlet's words ignores their deeper religious significance, and offers only a meaningless redundancy as a substitute.

> but heaven hath pleas'd it so,
> To punish me with this, and this with me,
> That I must be their scourge and minister.

We may paraphrase thus: Heaven has contrived this killing as a means of punishing us both and as a means of indicating to me that I must be its scourge and minister.

One need only dig down to this bare meaning to reveal how little the basic ideas have really been explained. Three difficult questions immediately assert themselves. Why was Heaven punishing Hamlet by making him the instrument of Polonius' death? Why does this punishment place him in the position of scourge and minister? What is the difference, if any, between scourge and minister? These are best answered, perhaps, in inverse order. The standard religious concept of the time was that God intervened in human affairs in two ways, internally and externally. Internally, God could punish sin by arousing the conscience of an individual to a sense of grief and remorse, which might in extraordinary cases grow so acute as to lead to madness. Externally, God worked through inanimate, or at least sub-human objects, through the forces of Nature, and through the agency of human beings. God's vengeance might strike a criminal by causing a sudden and abnormal mortal sickness, by sinking him in a squall at sea, by hitting him over the head with a falling timber, by leading him accidentally into a deep quicksand or unseen pool. The Elizabethans, if there was any suspected reason, were inclined to see God's hand in most such accidents. But sometimes Heaven punished crime by human agents, and it was standard belief that for this purpose God chose for His instruments those who were already so steeped in crime as to be past salvation. This was not only a principle of economy, but a means of freeing God from the impossible assumption that He would deliberately corrupt innocence. When a human agent was selected to be the instrument of God's vengeance, and the act of vengeance on the guilty necessitated the performance by the agent of a crime, like murder, only a man already damned for his sins was selected, and he was called a scourge.[3]

Any man who knew himself to be such a scourge knew both his function and his fate: his powers were not his own. Taking the long view, no matter how much he could glory in the triumphs of the present, his position was not an enviable one. Any human agent used by God to visit wrath and to scourge evil by evil was already condemned. This idea is clearly stated at the end of Fletcher's *Maid's Tragedy:*

> on lustful kings
> Unlook'd-for sudden deaths from God are sent;
> But curs'd is he that is their instrument.

When Hamlet called himself a scourge of Heaven, it is inconceivable that the Elizabethan audience did not know what he meant, and that Hamlet did not realize to the full what he was saying.

Although some writers, as in Fortescue's translation *The Forest,* [4] used scourge and minister interchangeably, there was a general tendency to distinguish them. The references in the concordance show, for our purposes, that Shakespeare always means minister in a good sense unless he specifies that the minister is of hell. A minister of God, in contrast to a scourge, is an agent who directly performs some good. In this sense, heavenly spirits are ministers of grace, as Hamlet calls them. The good performed by a human minister, however, may be some positive good in neutral or in good circumstances, or it may be some good which acts as a direct retribution for evil by overthrowing it and setting up a positive good in its place. The distinction between minister and scourge, thus, lies in two respects. First, a retributive minister may visit God's wrath on sin but only as the necessary final act to the overthrow of evil, whereas a scourge visits wrath alone, the delayed good to rest in another's hands. To take a rough and ready example, Richard III was thought of as a scourge for England, the final agent of God's vengeance for the deposition and murder of the anointed Richard II; but the good wishes of the ghosts make young Henry Richmond, in Raleigh's description, "the immediate instrument of God's justice," that is, a minister who will bring to a close God's wrath by exacting public justice in battle on the tyrant Richard, this triumph to be followed by a reign of peace and glory under the Tudor dynasty. In the second respect, as a contrast to the evil and damned scourge, if a minister's duty is to exact God's punishment or retribution as an act of good, his hands will not be stained with crime. If in some sense he is the cause of the criminal's death, the means provided him by Heaven will lie in some act of public justice, or of vengeance, rather than in criminal private revenge.

We are now in a position to examine Hamlet's "scourge and minister." We must recognize that the Ghost's command, though not explicit, was at first interpreted by Hamlet as a call to an act of private blood-revenge. Yet there is no getting around the fact that to an Elizabethan audience this was a criminal act of blood, not to be condoned by God, and therefore represented a particularly agonizing position for a tragic hero to be placed in. If Hamlet hopes to right the wrong done him and his father, and to ascend the throne of Denmark with honor, he must contrive a public vengeance which will demonstrate him to be a minister of Heaven's justice. Yet the secret murder of his father, so far as he can see, prevents all hope of public justice; and therefore the circumstances appear to him to enforce a criminal private revenge even after he realizes that he has been supernaturally appointed as minister. The enormous contrast between Hamlet's first promise to sweep to his revenge and his concluding, "The time is out of joint. O cursed spite,/ That ever I was born to set it right," has often been remarked, but not sufficiently against this background. Moreover, it has not been well considered that if the Ghost is a spirit of health, it could not escape from purgatory under its own volition in order to influence affairs on earth. Since divine permission alone could free the Ghost to revisit the earth, the Ghost's demand for the external punishment of Claudius, and its prophecy of the internal punishment of Gertrude, is not alone a personal call but in effect the transmission of a divine command, appointing Hamlet as God's agent to punish the specific criminal, Claudius.

With the final line of *The Maid's Tragedy* in our ears—"But curs'd is he that is their instrument"—we may see with full force the anomalous position Hamlet conceives for himself: is he to be the private-revenger scourge *or* the public-revenger minister? If scourge, he will make his own opportunities, will revenge murder with murder, and by this means visit God's wrath on corruption. If minister, God will see to it that a proper opportunity is offered in some way that will keep him clear from crime, one which will preserve him to initiate a good rule over Denmark. This crux for Hamlet has not been really pointed up, in part because Shakespeare had no need to make it explicit for his own audience.

As a consequence, Hamlet at the start finds himself in this peculiarly depressing position. He has been set aside from other human beings as an agent of God to set right the disjointed times, and he may reasonably assume from the circumstances of the ghostly visitation that he is a minister. Every private emotion urges him to a personal revenge of blood as the only means of solving his problem, and this revenge seems enforced by the secrecy of the original crime. But if he acts thus, he will be anticipating God's will, which in its good time will provide the just opportunity. If he anticipates and revenges, he risks damnation. If he does not revenge, he must torture himself with his seeming incompetence. In moments of the deepest depression, it could be natural for doubts to arise as to his role, and whether because of his "too too sullied flesh" he may not in fact have been appointed as a scourge, in which case his delay is indeed cowardly. Finally, there arises the important doubt whether the Ghost has been a demon to delude him into damning his soul by the murder of an innocent man, or indeed an agent of Heaven appointing him to an act of justice.

With these considerations in mind, the two months' delay between the Ghost's visitation and the next appearance of Hamlet in Act II may seem to have more validity than certain rather bloodthirsty critics will allow. I suggest that this delay, which Shakespeare never explicitly motivates, was caused not alone by rising doubts of the Ghost, or by the physical difficulties of getting at Claudius, or by the repugnance of a sensitive young man to commit an act of murder, or by his examining the circumstances so over-scrupulously as to become lost in the mazes of thought, motive, and doubt; but instead as much as anything by Hamlet as minister waiting on the expected opportunity which should be provided him, and not finding it.[5] The strain is, of course, tremendous, and it gives rise not only to his depressed musing on life and death in "To be or not to be" but also to the self-castigation of "O what a rogue and peasant slave." The corruption of the world, of men and women, and of Denmark with its interfering Polonius, its complaisant Ophelia, its traitorous Rosencrantz and Guildenstern whose love has been bought away from their schoolfellow—but especially of Denmark's source of corruption, its murderer-King and lustful, incestuous Queen—seem to cry out for scourging. To satisfy at least one question, he contrives the mousetrap and secures his answer, in the process revealing himself. And immediately an opportunity is given him for private revenge in the prayer scene, but one so far different from divinely appointed public vengeance that Heaven would never have provided it for its minister, a sign that the time is not yet. He passes on, racking himself with blood-thirsty promises, and—no longer trusting to Heaven's delays—impulsively takes the next action upon himself. He kills Polonius, thinking him the King. He repents, but does not expect his repentance to alter the scales of justice. Heaven, it is clear, has punished him for anticipating by his own deed the opportunity that was designed for the future. The precise form of the punishment consists in the fact that in killing, he has slain the wrong man; and the fact that it was Polonius and not the King behind the arras is the evidence for Heaven's punishment. He has irretrievably stained his hands with innocent blood by his usurping action, and foreseeing Heaven withheld his proper victim as its punishment.[6]

As I interpret it, therefore, Hamlet is not only punished *for* the murder of Polonius but *with* his murder, since Polonius was not his assigned victim; hence this fact is the evidence for Heaven's displeasure at his private revenge. The punishment *for* the murder will come, as indeed it does: it is this incident which for the Elizabethan audience motivated the justice of the tragic catastrophe and makes the closet scene the climax of the play.[7] Hamlet's words show his own recognition that he has in part made himself a scourge by the mistaken murder; and I suggest that it is his acceptance of this part of his total role that leads him to send Rosencrantz and Guildenstern so cheerfully, at least on the surface, to their doom. In his mind they are of the essence of the court's corruption under Claudius. They are adders fanged.

When next we see Hamlet, after the interlude of the graveyard scene, a manifest change has taken place. When he left for England, as shown by his "How all occasions do inform against me" soliloquy, he was still torn by his earlier dilemma of somehow reconciling the combat of his private emotions for revengeful action against the restraint of waiting on divine will. But it appears to him that very shortly Heaven reversed its course and actively demonstrated its guidance by preserving his life from the King's plot and returning him to Denmark, short-circuiting the delay of an English adventure. The conflict has certainly been resolved, and it is a different Hamlet indeed who tells Horatio that "There's a divinity that shapes our ends,/Rough-hew them how we will." He directly imputes his unsealing of the commission to heavenly prompting, and Heaven was even ordinant in providing him with his father's signet to reseal the papers. The pirates, it is clear, were only the natural culmination of Heaven's intervention on his side to bring him back to Denmark for the long-withheld vengeance.

When he recapitulates his wrongs, a new and quite different item is appended. It is true that Claudius, as he says, has killed his father, whored his mother, popped in between the election and his hopes, and has even attempted Hamlet's life by treacherous device. He demands for these, "Is't not perfect conscience/To quit him with this arm?" And then, significantly, he adds, "And is't not to be damn'd/To let this canker of our nature come/To further evil?" This is a note not heard before, an argument which would be used not by a private revenger but by one seeking public vengeance and justice. It says in effect: knowing what I know now, especially in this attempt on my life, I should be an accessory before the fact, and thus equally guilty with Claudius, if by further delay I permit him to enact more crimes. I should be directly responsible for further evil effects, and therefore I must see that his crimes are stopped.

Shakespeare here, as elsewhere, gives Hamlet no precise plan. But the note of confidence, not hitherto heard, is of the utmost importance. Before, when the ways of God were not at all apparent to his mind, we had "O what a rogue and peasant slave," or "How all occasions do inform against me." Now he says to Horatio, "The interim is mine," serene in trust that divine providence will guide him. Critics have noted this end to self-recrimination and conflict but have thought it odd that his confidence was based on no definite plan of action. Properly viewed, that is the precise point and it is one of great importance. His lack of plan and thus his insistence on providence arises from his confidence in Heaven. This is not lip-service or religious commonplace, but the very heart of the matter.

Immediately, Claudius' counterplot begins and the fencing match is arranged. Hamlet's assured feeling that he is only an instrument in the hands of God sustains him against the ominous portent of disaster that seizes on his heart. For he has learned his lesson from the results of killing Polonius. "There's a special providence in the fall of a sparrow," he says to Horatio; "if it be not now, yet it will come"; and, finally, the summation, "The readiness is all."

From the Elizabethan point of view, divine providence works out the catastrophe with justice. The plotters are hoist by their own villainous schemes; and then, triumphantly, the opportunity is given Hamlet to kill Claudius in circumstances which relieve him from immortal penalty for blood. By stage doctrine he must die for the slaying of Polonius, and, more doubtfully, for that of Rosencrantz and Guildenstern perhaps, the first in which he was inadvertently and the second consciously a scourge; and that penalty is being exacted. Since he cannot now ascend the throne over Claudius' body, all possible self-interest is removed. He has not plotted Claudius' death in cold blood, but seized an opportunity which under no circumstances he could have contrived by blood-revenge, to kill as a dying act of public justice a manifest and open murderer, exposed by the death of Gertrude, while himself suffering the pangs of death as his victim. The restitution of right lies only in him. Despite the terrible action of his forcing the poisoned cup between the King's teeth, Shakespeare takes great pains to remove the blood guilt from Hamlet by the expiation of his own death, and to indicate that the open killing was a ministerial act of public justice accomplished under the only possible circumstances. Hamlet's death is sufficient to expiate that of Polonius in the past and of Laertes in the present. With Christian charity Hamlet accepts Laertes' repentance and forgiveness accompanied by the prayer that "Mine and my father's death come not upon thee" in the future life; and in turn he prays that Heaven will make Laertes free from the guilt of his own. Finally, Horatio's blessing, "Flights of angels sing thee to thy rest," are words of benediction for a minister of providence who died through anticipating heavenly justice but, like Samson, was never wholly cast off for his tragic fault and in the end was honored by fulfilling divine plan in expiatory death. In more ways than one, but not necessarily more than he meant by his prophecy, Hamlet kept his promise for Polonius, "I will answer well the death I gave him."

Notes

1. As in Marston's *Antonio's Revenge* and Fletcher's *Bloody Brother*. See also my *Elizabethan Revenge Tragedy* (Princeton Univ. Press, 1940), pp. 11-12, 39-40.

2. *Elizabethan Revenge Tragedy,* p. 9.

3. Roy Battenhouse, *Marlowe's "Tamburlaine"* (Vanderbilt Univ. Press, 1941), pp. 13-15, 108-113.

4. See Battenhouse, p. 13, for a typical quotation.

5.   Strongly corroborative is the evidence of Tourneur's *Atheist's Tragedy,* a play manifestly influenced by *Hamlet* and one which carries this situation to its logical conclusion.

6.   That Heaven was behind all acts of reward or punishment is so much an article of Elizabethan tragic doctrine as to be instantly accepted at its face value by the audience without scrupulous enquiry into the hidden workings by which Heaven produced the results. Nor is it likely that Shakespeare worried much about the exact method or implications of this working in the situation in question. Heaven could readily order the ironic accident which, as a punishment, placed Polonius rather than Claudius behind the arras. However, with the proviso that there is no need to believe that Shakespeare or his audience sought out the implications in full detail, it may be remarked that the action of Heaven was theologically explicable. The crucial point is the distinction between foreknowledge and fore-ordination. It cannot be taken that Heaven fore-ordained that Hamlet should disobey and impulsively attempt revenge before Heaven had provided the opportunity and means for exhibiting the act as one of justice. On the other hand, one cannot limit the knowledge of God; and thus Heaven could foresee that Hamlet would perform this action. Conditional upon this foreknowledge, therefore, Heaven orders it so that Polonius substitutes for Claudius. The actions of Heaven conditional upon God's knowledge of the future are theologically quite different from Heaven's preordination, which wills certains events to take place.

7.   This point needs emphasis because the prayer scene is still occasionally cited as the climax. The climax is that scene in a play in which an action occurs which tips the scales for or against the fate of the protagonist in terms of the future action. The arguments for the prayer scene as the climax are superficial, for they turn only on the point that Hamlet suffers death in the catastrophe because he spared Claudius in this scene. Two considerations are always present in a tragedy. First, the climax must directly produce a train of action that leads to the catastrophe. Second, if we may briefly define tragedy as a series of morally determinate actions, the climactic scene must involve a morally determined action which justifies the tragic catastrophe to come. If we survey the prayer scene according to these two considerations, we may see that neither applies. Plotwise, no train of action results from the sparing of Claudius. Claudius' own plan, the English voyage with its deadly ending, has already been set in motion, but is to prove abortive. On the contrary, as a direct result of the killing of Polonius the plot picks up Laertes as his revenger. Claudius' own plan of the poisoned cup backfires and is one of the means for his downfall, but Laertes' plan succeeds and is the immediate cause of Hamlet's death. By a direct and continuous line of action the catastrophe goes back to the killing of Polonius. What the action of the play would have been like if Laertes had not had the occasion to revenge the death of his father, we cannot tell. This in itself is enough to remove the prayer scene from consideration as the climax from the point of view of the plot. As for the second requirement—the morally determinate action—if Hamlet's sparing of Claudius is to be a tragic error of such magnitude as to make his subsequent death an act of justice, we must take it that he should have killed Claudius at prayer. This would require the audience to be convinced that Hamlet's decision was wrong in the light of his belief that Claudius was in a state of grace. It is difficult to see how such a theory could be defended. On the other hand, if the ethical climax is to coincide with the plot climax, as it should, we are forced into examining the killing of Polonius as a morally determinated action. Greek tragedy might have made of this scene a study of simple fatal error, something like Oedipus slaying his father, and drawn the moral of the ways in which fate interferes with human life. But the Elizabethan is not the Greek drama, and the English tragic writers would have agreed with Milton's God who pronounces, "What I will is Fate." The general Christian framework of Elizabethan tragic ethics demands that the slaying of Polonius be more than an unlucky accident. So far as I can see, the only way to give it a moral determinism is to argue, as I do, that it was a real error for Hamlet to attempt his private revenge at this time when Heaven had put him in a position of a minister for whom public justice would be arranged at Heaven's own pleasure. The tragic error consists in the fact that Hamlet's emotional

drive is too strong to permit him to wait upon what appears to him to be Heaven's extraordinary delay. Paradoxically, therefore, the tragic fact is not Hamlet's delay except for its effect upon his cumulative impatience, but instead his attempt at action. Once again, Tourneur's *Atheist's Tragedy* must be cited, with its protagonist who is in the same fix but who successfully overcomes the temptation to anticipate Heaven and who therefore survives.

Selected Criticisms

I believe the character of Hamlet may be traced to Shakespeare's deep and accurate science in mental philosophy. Indeed, that this character must have some connection with the common fundamental laws of our nature may be assumed from the fact that Hamlet has been the darling of every country in which the literature of England has been fostered. In order to understand him, it is essential that we should reflect on the constitution of our own minds. Man is distinguished from the brute animals in proportion as thought prevails over sense; but in the healthy processes of the mind, a balance is constantly maintained between the impressions from outward objects and the inward operations of the intellect; for if there be an overbalance in the contemplative faculty, man thereby becomes the creature of mere meditation, and loses his natural power of action. Now, one of Shakespeare's modes of creating characters is to conceive any one intellectual or moral faculty in morbid excess, and then to place himself, Shakespeare, thus mutilated or diseased, under given circumstances. In Hamlet he seems to have wished to exemplify the moral necessity of a due balance between our attention to the objects of our senses and our meditation on the working of our minds—an *equilibrium* between the real and the imaginary worlds. In Hamlet this balance is disturbed; his thoughts and the images of his fancy are far more vivid than his actual perceptions, and his very perceptions, instantly passing through the *medium* of his contemplations, acquire, as they pass, a form and a colour not naturally their own. Hence we see a great, an almost enormous, intellectual activity, and a proportionate aversion to real action consequent upon it, with all its symptoms and accompanying qualities. This character Shakespeare places in circumstances under which it is obliged to act on the spur of the moment: Hamlet is brave and careless of death; but he vacillates from sensibility, and procrastinates from thought, and loses the power of action in the energy of resolve. Thus it is that this tragedy presents a direct contrast to that of *Macbeth*: the one proceeds with the utmost slowness, the other with a crowded and breathless rapidity.

Samuel Taylor Coleridge

The grounds of *Hamlet's* failure [as a work of art] are not immediately obvious. Mr. Robertson [J. M. Robertson, an American critic] is undoubtedly correct in concluding that the essential emotion of the play is the feeling of a son towards a guilty mother. . . . This, however, is by no means the whole story. It is not merely the 'guilt of a mother' that cannot be handled as Shakespeare handled the suspicion of Othello, the infatuation of Antony, or the pride of Coriolanus. The subject might conceivably have expanded into a tragedy like these, intelligible, self-complete, in the sunlight. *Hamlet,* like the sonnets is full of some stuff that the writer could not drag to light, contemplate, or manipulate into art. And when we search for this feeling, we find it, as in the sonnets, very difficult to localize. You cannot point to it in the speeches; indeed, if you examine the two famous soliloquies you see the versification of Shakespeare, but a content which might be claimed by another, perhaps by the author of the *Revenge of Bussy d'Ambois,* Act V. Sc. 1. We find Shakespeare's *Hamlet* not in the action, not in any quotations that we might select, so much as in an unmistakable tone which is unmistakably not in the earlier play.

The only way of expressing emotion in the form of art is by finding an 'objective correlative'; in other words, a set of objects, a situation, a chain of events which shall be the formula of that *particular* emotion; such that when the external facts, which must terminate in sensory experience, are given, the emotion is immediately evoked. If you examine any of Shakespeare's more successful tragedies, you will find this exact equivalence; you will find that the state of mind of Lady Macbeth walking in her sleep has been communicated to you by a skilful accumulation of imagined sensory impressions; the words of Macbeth on hearing of his wife's death strike us as if, given the sequence of events, these words were automatically released by the last event in the series. The artistic 'inevitability' lies in this complete adequacy of the external to the emotion; and this is precisely what is deficient in *Hamlet.* Hamlet (the man) is dominated by an emotion which is inexpressible, because it is in *excess* of the facts as they appear. And the supposed identity of Hamlet with his author is genuine to this point: that Hamlet's bafflement at the absence of objective equivalent to his feelings is a prolongation of the bafflement of his creator in the face of his artistic problem. Hamlet is up against the difficulty that his disgust is occasioned by his mother, but that his mother is not an adequate equivalent for it; his disgust envelops and exceeds her. It is thus a feeling which he cannot understand; he cannot objectify it, and it therefore remains to poison life and obstruct action. None of the possible actions can satisfy it; and nothing that Shakespeare can do with the plot can express Hamlet for him. And it must be noticed that the very nature of the *données* [fundamental ideas] of the problem precludes objective equivalence. To have heightened the criminality of Gertrude would have been to provide the formula for a totally different emotion in Hamlet; it is just *because* her character is so negative and insignificant that she arouses in Hamlet the feeling which she is incapable of representing.

The 'madness' of Hamlet lay to Shakespeare's hand; in the earlier play a simple ruse, and to the end, we may presume, understood as a ruse by the audience. For Shakespeare it is less than madness and more than feigned. The levity of Hamlet, his repetition of phrase, his puns, are not part of a deliberate plan of dissimulation, but a form of emotional relief. In the character Hamlet it is the buffoonery of an emotion which he cannot express in art. The intense feeling, ecstatic or terrible, without an object or exceeding its object, is something which every person of sensibility has known; it is doubtless a subject of study for pathologists. It often occurs in adolescence: the ordinary person puts these feelings to sleep, or trims down his feelings to fit the business world; the artist keeps them alive by his ability to intensify the world to his emotions.

T. S. Eliot

I believe that we read Hamlet's speeches with interest chiefly because they describe so well a certain spiritual region through which most of us have passed and anyone in his circumstances might be expected to pass, rather than because of our concern to understand how and why this particular man entered it. I foresee an objection on the ground that I am thus really admitting his 'character' in the only sense that matters and that all characters whatever could be equally well talked away by the method I have adopted. But I do really find a distinction. . . . In Shakespeare himself I find Beatrice to be a character who could not be thus dissolved. We are interested not in some vision seen through her eyes, but precisely in the wonder of her being the girl she is. A comparison of the sayings we remember from her part with those we remember from Hamlet's brings out the contrast. On the one hand, 'I wonder that you will still be talking, Signior Benedick', 'There was a star danced and under that I was born', 'Kill Claudio'; on the other, 'The undiscovered country, from whose bourne no traveller returns', 'Use every man after his desert, and who should 'scape whipping?', 'The rest is silence.' Particularly noticeable is the passage where Hamlet professes to be describing his own character. 'I am myself indifferent honest, but yet I could accuse me of such things that it were better my mother had not borne me; I am very proud, revengeful, ambitious'. It is, of course, possible to devise some theory which explains these self-accusations in terms of character. But long before we have done so the real significance of the lines has taken possession of our imagination for ever. 'Such fellows as I' does not mean 'such fellows as Goethe's Hamlet, or Coleridge's Hamlet, or any Hamlet': it means *men* — creatures shapen in sin and conceived in iniquity — and the vast, empty visions of them 'crawling between earth and heaven' is what really counts and really carries the burden of the play.

It is often cast in the teeth of the great critics that each in painting *Hamlet* has drawn a portrait of himself. How if they were right? I would go a long way to meet Beatrice or Falstaff or Mr Jonathan Oldbuck or Disraeli's Lord Monmouth. I would not cross the room to meet Hamlet. It would never be necessary. He is always where I am. The method of the whole play is much nearer to Mr Eliot's own method in poetry than Mr Eliot suspects. Its true hero is man — haunted man — man with his mind on the frontier of two worlds, man unable to either quite to reject or quite to admit the supernatural, man struggling to get something done as man has struggled from the beginning, yet incapable of achievement because of his inability to understand either himself or his fellows or the real quality of the universe which has produced him. To be sure, some hints of more particular motives for Hamlet's delay are every now and then fadged up to silence our questions, just as some show of motives is offered for the Duke's temporary abdication in *Measure for Measure.* In both cases it is only scaffolding or machinery. To mistake these were *succedanea* [substitutions] for the real play and to try to work them up into a coherent psychology is the great error. I once had a whole batch of School Certificate answers on the "Nun's Priest's Tale' by boys whose form-master was apparently a breeder of poultry. Everything that Chaucer had said in describing Chauntecleer and Pertelote was treated by them simply and solely as evidence about the precise breed of these two birds. And, I must admit, the result was very interesting. They proved beyond doubt that Chauntecleer was very different from our modern specialized strains and much closer to the Old English 'barn-door fowl'. But I couldn't help feeling that they had missed something. I believe our attention to Hamlet's 'character' in the usual sense misses almost as much.

Perhaps I should rather say that it *would* miss as much if our behaviour when we are actually reading were not wiser than our criticism in cold blood. The critics, or most of them, have at any rate kept constantly before us the knowledge that in this play there is greatness and mystery. They were never entirely wrong. Their error, in my view, was to put the mystery in the wrong place—in Hamlet's motives rather than in that darkness which enwraps Hamlet and the whole tragedy and all who read or watch it. It is a mysterious play in the sense of being a play about mystery. Mr. Eliot suggests that 'more people have thought *Hamlet* a work of art because they found it interesting, than have found it interesting because it is a work of art'. When he wrote that sentence he must have been very near to what I believe to be the truth. The play is, above all else, *interesting.* But artistic failure is not in itself interesting, nor often interesting in any way: artistic success always is. To interest is the first duty of art; no other excellences will even begin to compensate for failure in this, and very serious faults will be covered by this, as by charity. The hypothesis that this play interests by being good and not by being bad has therefore the first claim on our consideration. The burden of proof rests on the other side. Is not the fascinated interest of the critics most naturally explained by supposing that this is the precise effect the play was written to produce? They may be finding the mystery in the wrong place; but the fact that they can never leave *Hamlet* alone, the continual groping, the sense, unextinguished by over a century of failures, that we have here something of inestimable importance, is surely the best evidence that the real and lasting mystery of our human situation has been greatly depicted.

C. S. Lewis

Claudius' virtues . . . are manifest. So are his faults—his original crime, his skill in the less admirable kind of policy, treachery, and intrigue. But I would point clearly that, in the movement of the play, his faults are forced on him, and he is distinguished by creative and wise action, a sense of purpose, benevolence, a faith in himself and those around him, by love of his Queen:

> . . . and for myself—
> My virtue or my plague, be it either which—
> She's so conjunctive to my life and soul,
> That, as the star moves not but in his sphere,
> I could not but by her.

(Act IV, Sc. 7, 12-16)

In short he is very human. Now these are the very qualities Hamlet lacks. Hamlet is inhuman. He has seen through humanity. And this inhuman cynicism, however justifiable in this case on the plane of causality and individual responsibility, is a deadly and venomous thing. Instinctively the creatures of earth, Laertes, Polonius, Ophelia, Rosencrantz and Guildenstern, league themselves with Claudius: they are of his kind. They sever themselves from Hamlet. Laertes sternly warns Ophelia against her intimacy with Hamlet, so does Polonius. They are in fact, all leagued against him, they are puzzled by him or fear him: he has no friend except Horatio, and Horatio, after the Ghost scenes, becomes a queer shadowy character who rarely gets beyond 'E'en so, my lord', 'My lord_____', and such-like phrases. The other persons are firmly drawn, in the round, creatures of flesh and blood. But Hamlet is not of flesh and blood, he is a spirit of penetrating intellect and cynicism and misery, without faith in himself or anyone else, murdering his love of Ophelia, on the brink of insanity, taking delight in cruelty, torturing Claudius, wringing his mother's heart, a poison in the midst of the healthy bustle of the court. He is a superman among men. And he is a superman because he has walked and held converse with death, and his consciousness works in terms of death and the negation of cynicism. He has seen the truth, not alone of Denmark, but of humanity, of the universe: and the truth is evil. Thus Hamlet is an element of evil in the state of Denmark. The poison of his

118

mental existence spreads outwards among things of flesh and blood, like acid eating into metal. They are helpless before his very inactivity and fall one after the other, like victims of an infectious disease. They are strong with the strength of health—but the demon of Hamlet's mind is a stronger thing than they. Futilely they try to get him out of their country; anything to get rid of him, he is not safe. But he goes with a cynical smile, and is no sooner gone than he is back again in their midst, meditating in graveyards, at home with death. Not till it has slain all, is the demon that grips Hamlet satisfied. And last it slays Hamlet himself:

> The spirit that I have seen
> May be the devil . . .
>
> (Act II, Sc. 2, 573-74)

It was the devil of the knowledge of death, which possesses Hamlet and drives him from misery and pain to increasing bitterness, cynicism, murder, and madness. He has indeed bought converse with his father's spirit at the price of enduring and spreading Hell on earth. But however much we may sympathize with Ophelia, with Polonius, Rosencrantz, Guildenstern, the Queen, and Claudius, there is one reservation to be made. It is Hamlet who is right. What he says and thinks of them is true, and there is no fault in his logic. His own mother is indeed faithless, and the prettiness of Ophelia does in truth enclose a spirit as fragile and untrustworthy as her earthly beauty; Polonius is 'a foolish prating knave'; Rosencrantz and Guildenstern are time-servers and flatterers; Claudius, whose benevolence hides the guilt of murder, is, by virtue of that fact, 'a damned smiling villain'. In the same way the demon of cynicism which is in the mind of the poet and expresses itself in the figures of this play, has always this characteristic: it is right. One cannot argue with the cynic. It is unwise to offer him battle. For in the warfare of logic it will be found that he has all the guns.

G. Wilson Knight

Is it possible to conceive an experience more desolating to a man such as we have seen Hamlet to be; and is its result anything but perfectly natural? It brings bewildered horror, then loathing, then despair of human nature. His whole mind is poisoned. He can never see Ophelia in the same light again: she is a woman, and his mother is a woman: if she mentions the word 'brief' to him, the answer drops from his lips like venom, 'as woman's love.' The last words of the soliloquy, which is *wholly* concerned with this subject, are,

> But break, my heart, for I must hold my tongue!

He can do nothing. He must lock in his heart, not any suspicion of his uncle that moves obscurely there, but that horror and loathing; and if his heart ever found relief, it was when those feelings, mingled with the love that never died out in him, poured themselves forth in a flood as he stood in his mother's chamber beside his father's marriage-bed.

If we still wonder, and ask why the effect of this shock should be so tremendous, let us observe that *now* the conditions have arisen under which Hamlet's highest endowments, his moral sensibility and his genius, become his enemies. A nature morally blunter would have felt even so dreadful a revelation less keenly. A slower and more limited and positive mind might not have extended so widely through its world the disgust and disbelief that have entered it. . . . But Hamlet has the imagination which, for evil as well as good, feels and sees all things in one. Thought is the element of his life, and his thought is infected. He cannot prevent himself from probing and lacerating the wound in his soul. One idea, full of peril, holds him fast, and he cries out in agony at it, but is impotent to free himself ('Must I remember?' 'Let me not think on't'). And when, with the fading of his passion, the vividness of this idea abates, it does so only to leave behind a boundless weariness and a sick longing for death.

And this is the time which his fate chooses. In this hour of uttermost weakness, this sinking of his whole being towards annihilation, there comes on him, bursting the bounds of the natural world with a shock of astonishment and terror, the revelation of his mother's adultery and his father's murder, and, with this, the demand on him, in the name of everything dearest and most sacred, to arise and act. And for a moment, though his brain reels and totters, his soul leaps up in passion to answer this demand. But it comes too late. It does but strike home the last rivet in the melancholy which holds him bound.

> The time is out of joint! O cursed spite
> That ever I was born to set it right,—

so he mutters within an hour of the moment when he vowed to give his life to the duty of revenge; and the rest of the story exhibits his vain efforts to fulfil this duty, his unconscious self-excuses and unavailing self-reproaches, and the tragic results of his delay.

'Melancholy,' I said, not dejection, nor yet insanity. That Hamlet was not far from insanity is very probable. His adoption of the pretence of madness may well have been due in part to fear of the reality; to an instinct of self-preservation, a fore-feeling that the pretence would enable him to give some utterance to the load that pressed on his heart and brain, and a fear that he would be unable altogether to repress such utterance. And if the pathologist calls his state melancholia, and even proceeds to determine its species, I see nothing to object to in that; I am grateful to him for emphasising the fact that Hamlet's melancholy was no mere common depression of spirits; and I have no doubt that many readers of the play would understand it better if they read an account of melancholia in a work on mental diseases. If we like to use the word 'disease' loosely, Hamlet's condition may truly be called diseased. No exertion of will could have dispelled it. Even if he had been able at once to do the bidding of the Ghost he would doubt-less have still remained for some time under the cloud. It would be ab-surdly unjust to call *Hamlet* a study of melancholy, but it contains such a study.

But this melancholy is something very different from insanity, in anything like the usual meaning of that word. No doubt it might de-velop into insanity. The longing for death might become an irresistible impulse to self-destruction; the disorder of feeling and will might extend to sense and intellect; delusions might arise; and the man might become, as we say, incapable and irresponsible. But Hamlet's melan-choly is some way from this condition. It is a totally different thing from the madness which he feigns; and he never, when alone or in company with Horatio alone, exhibits the signs of that madness. Nor is the dramatic use of this melancholy, again, open to the objections which would justly be made to the portrayal of an insanity which brought the hero to a tragic end. The man who suffers as Hamlet suf-fers—and thousands go about their business suffering thus in greater or less degree—is considered irresponsible neither by other people nor by himself: he is only too keenly conscious of his responsibility. He is therefore, so far, quite capable of being a tragic agent, which an insane person, at any rate according to Shakespeare's practice, is not. And finally, Hamlet's state is not one which a healthy mind is unable suf-ficiently to imagine. It is probably not further from average exper-ience, nor more difficult to realise, than the great tragic passions of Othello, Antony or Macbeth.

A. C. Bradley

We are compelled then to take the position that there is some cause for Hamlet's vacillation which has not yet been fathomed. If this lies neither in his incapacity for action in general, nor in the inordinate difficulty of the particular task in question, then it must of necessity lie in the third possibility—namely, in some special feature of the task that renders it repugnant to him. This conclusion, that Hamlet at heart does not want to carry out the task, seems so obvious that it is hard to see how any open-minded reader of the play could avoid making it . . .

For some deep-seated reason, which is to him unacceptable, Ham-let is plunged into anguish at the thought of his father being replaced in his mother's affections by someone else. It is as if his devotion to his mother had made him so jealous for her affection that he had found it hard enough to share this even with his father and could not endure to share it with still another man. Against this thought, however, suggestive as it is, may be urged three objections. First, if it were in itself a full statement of the matter, Hamlet would have been aware of the jealousy, whereas we have concluded that the mental process we are seeking is hidden from him. Secondly, we see in it no evidence of the arousing of an old and forgotten memory. And, thirdly, Hamlet is being deprived by Claudius of no greater share in the Queen's affection than he had been by his own father, for the two brothers made exactly similar claims in this respect—namely, those of a loved husband. The last-named objection, however, leads us to the heart of the situation. How if, in fact, Hamlet had in years gone by, as a child, bitterly resented having had to share his mother's affection even with his own father, had regarded him as a rival, and had secretly wished him out of the way so that he might enjoy undisputed and undisturbed the monopoly of that affection. If such thoughts had been present in his mind in childhood days they evidently would have been 'repressed', and all traces of them obliterated, by filial piety and other educative influences. The actual realization of his early wish in the death of his father at the hands of a jealous rival would then have stimulated into activity these 'repressed' memories, which would have produced, in the form of depression and other suffering, an obscure aftermath of his childhood's conflict. This is at all events the mechanism that is actually found in the real Hamlets who are investigated psychologically.

The explanation, therefore, of the delay and self-frustration exhibited in the endeavour to fulfil his father's demand for vengeance is that to Hamlet the thought of incest and parricide combined is too intolerable to be borne. One part of him tries to carry out the task, the other flinches inexorably from the thought of it. How fain would he blot it out in that 'bestial oblivion' which unfortunately for him his conscience condemns. He is torn and tortured in an insoluble inner conflict . . .

Ernest Jones

Bibliography

Alexander, Peter. *Hamlet: Father and Son*. Oxford: The Clarendon Press, 1955.

Bowers, Fredson. *Elizabethan Revenge Tragedy*. Princeton: Princeton University Press, 1940.

Bradley, A. C. *Shakespearean Tragedy*. 2nd edition. New York: St. Martin's Press, 1978.

Campbell, Lily B. *Shakespeare's Tragic Heroes: Slaves of Passion*. New York: Cambridge University Press, 1930.

Charney, M. *Style in Hamlet*. Princeton: Princeton University Press, 1969.

Coleridge, S. T. *Coleridge's Writings on Shakespeare,* ed. T. Hawkes. New York: G. P. Putnam's Sons, 1959.

Eliot, T. S. "Hamlet and His Problems," in *Selected Essays*. New York: Harcourt, Brace and World, 1950.

Fergusson, Francis. *The Idea of a Theatre*. Princeton: Princeton University Press, 1949.

Fisch, Harold. *Hamlet and the World*. New York: Ungar, 1971.

Granville-Barker, Harley. *Prefaces to Shakespeare*. 2 vols. Princeton: Princeton University Press, 1946-47.

Grebanier, B. *The Heart of Hamlet*. New York: Thomas Y. Crowell, 1960.

Harbage, Alfred. *Shakespeare: A Reader's Guide*. New York: Farrar, Straus and Co., 1963.

Jones, Ernest. *Hamlet and Oedipus*. New York: W. W. Norton, 1949.

Knight, G. W. *The Wheel of Fire*. Rev. ed. London: Metheun, 1949.

Knights, L. C. *An Approach to Hamlet*. London: Chatto and Windus, 1960.

Levin, Harry. *The Question of Hamlet*. Oxford: Oxford University Press, 1959.

Madariaga, Salvador de. *On Hamlet*. London: Hollis and Carter, 1948.

Ribner, Irving. *Patterns in Shakespearean Tragedy*. London: Methuen, 1960.

Rosen, William. *Shakespeare and the Craft of Tragedy*. Cambridge: Harvard University Press, 1960.

Sanders, Leonard. *The Hamlet Warning*. New York: Scribner, 1976.

Schücking, L. L. *Character Problems in Shakespeare's Plays*. New York: H. Holt, 1922.

Tillyard, E. M. W. *Shakespeare's Problem Plays*. London: Chatto and Windus, 1951.

Traversi, Derek. *An Approach to Shakespeare*. New York: Doubleday, 1956.

Walker, Roy. *The Time Is Out of Joint*. London: A. Dakers, 1948.

Wilson, J. Dover. *What Happens in Hamlet*. New York: Macmillan, 1940.